Contents

Preface	7

Self Liberation Book One : Fear — 11

What is Fear
    Understanding Fear and Phobia — 13
Types of Fear
    Knowing natural and unnatural fears — 17
The six causes of Fear
    Know the cause and eradicate the effect — 23
Freedom from Fear : Part One
    Three steps that will weaken the roots of fear — 27
Freedom from Fear : Part Two
    Three steps that will make the tree of fear to fall — 31
The Fear Liberating Mantra
    I am God's property, no evil can touch me — 37
Liberation from the fear of Death
    How to kill the fear of death — 41
The Instant Way to be rid of Fear
    The power of imagination — 45
The Ultimate Way to be rid of Fear
    Take an oath that you will not die before your death — 49

Self Liberation Book Two : Worry — 53

What is Worry
    Understanding worry, anxiety, stress and panic — 55
The Invisible Way to be rid of Worry
    Prayer – The greatest power — *59*
The In-depth Way to be rid of Worry
    Stop worrying about worry — 62
The First Way to be rid of Worry
    The one hour worry cure technique — 65
The Second Way to be rid of Worry
    Desensitize yourself from worry — 68
The Third Way to be rid of Worry
    Three questions, three steps, one formula — 70
The Practical Way to be rid of Worry
    The law of average wrecks worry and destroys delusion — 73

The Illogical Way to be rid of Worry
    Learn To Laugh At Your Worries   76
The Intelligent Way to be rid of Worry
    The power of rational thinking   78
The Knowledgeable Way to be rid of Worry
    Know the irrefutable law of life   81
The Positive Way to be rid of Worry
    Your attitude determines your altitude   85
The Worry Liberation Mantra
    The problem that is not grave enough to slay me can only strengthen me   89
The Easiest Way to be rid of Worry
    Know your instinctive mind   93
The Final Way to be rid of Worry
    Increase your worries   97

Self Liberation Book Three : Anger   101

What is Anger
    Understanding anger and the defilements of the mind 103
Types of the Angry
    Find your type   109
Childhood and the Beginnings of Anger
    The responsible way to rid your child of anger   111
The Aware Way to be rid of Anger
    Understand the effects of anger   117
The Revolutionary Way to be rid of Anger
    Embrace, transform and use anger   123
The Knowledgeable Way to get freedom from Anger
    Know the cause, remove the effect   127
The Prepared Way to be rid of Anger
    Ten measures to get rid of anger before anger arises   133
The Coolest Way of calming Anger
    Prayer – The blessing of peace   137
Eight Quick fire Measures to calm the fire of Anger
    Temporary measures   139
Seven Sure Ways to get rid of Anger
    Permanent measures   143
The Ultimate Way to be rid of Anger
    The anger liberation mantra   151

Preface

Reading the first and last paragraph is recommended

Everyone in the world was living happily. There were no problems at all. Then one fine day, everyone in the world accepted an invitation to attend a marriage. The marriage was to happen between Fear and Worry. Illusion, the father of the bride and Depression, the mother of the bridegroom invited the solemn presence of everyone. The priest was Anger who completed the unholy alliance without thinking twice. Since then everyone has been visiting the couple daily and seeking counselling from the priest. They seem to see no way of living without them.

Looking at the devastating effects of fear, worry and anger in the present day world, the fable mentioned above could very much be true. Modern life is a life of stress, hurry and tight schedules. We are living in the age where the computers are married to the telephones, where moral values have taken a backseat and deadlines [not lifelines] set the course of the day. There is so much to be done, but no time to do it. This naturally results in fear, worry and anger. Wherever you look, you can see nothing but strife, conflict and grudges. In every direction, we see anxious, depressed and furious faces. Every place is blazing with fights, disputes and hatred. Brother is fighting against brother, son is tussling against father, daughter-in-law is quarrelling with mother-in-law, daughter is clashing against mother, son is bickering his mother, friend is battling against friend, neighbour is contending against neighbour...!

There have been many things said about fear, worry and anger. But yet the terrible threesome continue to plague every person, every home, every neighbourhood, every society, every office, every city, every state, every country. They continue to trouble because many things about fear, worry and anger remain unsaid. This book is an attempt to bring about the missing link in understanding them and banishing them from our lives forever.

Indeed many things have been said so far about fear, worry and anger; many things that only make us more afraid of fear, more anxious about worrying and furious about anger. In our research in India and abroad, before translating this book, we came across various books and programs on fear, worry and anger. All of them were problem statements. None of them offered practical solutions. The importance of this book is that it is a solution set that can be applied in everyday life. It contains multiple solutions against fear, worry and anger. While we were translating this book, we realized that this is the most comprehensive set of techniques or solutions on the troublesome three we have ever come across. We thank Sirshree for penning the Hindi original. It is a privilege to translate this wonderful book for English Lovers.

Krishna Iyer and Nitin Ahir

How to read this book :

1. Read the book end to end so that *you feel free from fear forever*, can *wage war with worry and win* and *accomplish the annihilation of anger adequately*.

2. Whenever fear, worry or anger strikes, then open any page of this book. Read whatever solution comes up. Contemplate on the solution. Implement the solution.

3. If you are distraught with fear, then start with book one. If you are troubled by worry, then book two is from where you can start. If you are furious with anger then book three will be the antidote.

4. There are three mantras given in the book, first to combat worry, the second to use against fear and third to abolish anger. Use these mantras in your day-to-day life. Reread those chapters (Chapter 6, book one, Chapter 12, book two and Chapter 11, book three) whenever it is important to remind yourself about these powerful mantras.

5. While reading this book, remind yourself that liberation in its truest sense is what one should attain. 'Self liberation from fear, worry and anger' is just a stepping stone.

Self Liberation

Book One : Fear

1 WHAT IS FEAR
Understanding Fear and Phobia

What is Fear

Fear is a response to an external threat, and usually produces changes in the sufferer's action and body. Generally, humans react to fear in three ways : fight, flight or freeze. We may muster up courage and fight the source of danger (fight); we may feel terrified and flee frantically to escape (flee); or become immobilized, motionless and mute (freeze). This book will give you the fourth way to win over fear.

Fear is misuse of man's imagination. Fear is a psychological disease. Fear emanates from man's ignorance. Fear is just a thought. Fear is an invention of human mind.

Once an epidemic (personified) was entering a village. The guard of the village asked the epidemic as to how many people it intended to kill. The epidemic replied that it had intentions of killing five hundred people. When the epidemic was returning back, the guard stopped it and accused it of lying. "You said five hundred, but you killed 1000 people." The epidemic replied, "I killed only five hundred. The other five hundred died fearing that they had the disease."

Such is the menace of fear. Anger, worry, hatred, greed, guilt and hopelessness are some of the harmful thoughts people carry. Fear tops the list. It can even be fatal.

Fear is a disease that, like a termite, destroys a person's life. Fear makes a person feel inferior. Fear itself is the root cause of most failures. The fear of failure sometimes leads a person even to commit suicide.

We unknowingly carry such a dangerous thing within us. We see people around us leading fearful lives. We learn of many tragic events through TV, newspapers etc., which take place only due to fear.

Phobia

Aggravated fear is termed as phobia. A phobia is an excessive, enduring fear of objects or situations that interferes with a person's normal life. Although they know their fear is irrational, people with phobias always try to avoid the source of their fear. Common phobias include fear of heights (acrophobia), fear of enclosed places (claustrophobia), fear of insects, snakes, or other animals, and fear of air travel.

Panic

Panic attacks are intense, overpowering surges of fear. Some people experience panic attacks - periods of quickly escalating intense fear and discomfort accompanied by physical symptoms such as rapid heartbeat, trembling, shortness of breath, dizziness or nausea. Because people with this extreme form of fear cannot predict when these attacks will strike, they worry about having more panic attacks and may limit their activities outside home.

A : Do you fear anyone?

B : No one except God.

A : Then you fear everyone.

TYPES OF FEAR
Knowing natural and unnatural fears

Identification and honest acceptance of one's fears is the first step towards winning over them. Following is a list of commonly found fears. Mark the fears that you have.

Fear of Unknown (death, darkness, etc.)

Fear of nature (flood, earthquake, etc.)

Fear of insecurity (old age, height, space, etc.)

Fear of people (teachers, doctors, boss, etc.)

Fear of Unknown

a) **Fear of darkness :** Darkness means lack of light. People who fear darkness cannot go into the kitchen to drink water in the night. They fear that there is someone unknown in the dark. Things get worse if they happened to watch a horror show on television.

b) **Fear of future :** Future is unknown and uncertain and thus people worry about it. Too much anxiety and worry about the future makes us fearful of the future.

c) **Fear of death :** The thought of death of someone near and dear or the thought of one's own death always causes fear in the minds of people. If a funeral procession is passing by, children are prevented from seeing it or are told to put their hand on their head, etc. Death, Ghosts, Spirits, Black Magic, etc. are unknown things. We fear these things due to ignorance. Life after death too is unknown and thus the thought of death makes people uneasy and insecure.

d) **Fear of God :** Fear of God prevails in many forms. Many believe that cutting hair on a certain day or eating sour food on a specific day, not accepting offerings, or not kneeling before a temple deity with due respect...all such things make God angry. These beliefs prevail because we do not know God and therefore end up believing the hearsay.

People ask, "Is God really there?"

Well, the answer is, "God alone is. Ascertain if you are there."

Fear of Nature

This fear includes fear of wild animals, fire, storms, water, lightning, earthquake, etc.

a) **Fear of animals :** Some women, if they come to know that there is a cockroach, lizard, etc. in their kitchen, will not enter the kitchen. Some will even go to the extent of declaring: "Take the lizard out of the house at once. Either the lizard will stay in this house or I." Fear of animals includes the fear of even pet animals like dogs, cats, etc.

b) **Fear of diseases/illness :** People hear or read the names of various new diseases every day and get frightened. These frightened people then search for symptoms of such diseases in themselves. If they find any, which they are sure to, they exaggerate it and start fearing that they have acquired the disease.

c) **Fear of water :** Many people fear water. Due to this fear, they do not enter swimming pools or ponds. They fear even going near water.

d) **Fear of open roads and open sky:** Some people fear open space. They have difficulty even when crossing highways.

e) **Fear of accident/blood:** Some people feel giddy when they see an accident or if they see blood.

Fear of insecurity

People feel insecure for various reasons:

a) **Fear of old age:** People fear being without work, being away from family and children and the perils that come with old age.

b) **Fear of heights:** Some people feel giddy when they look down from heights. They cannot even enjoy the roller coaster rides in amusement parks.

c) **Fear of closed places:** Some people fear closed places. They would rather use the stairs than take the elevator. They even hate to go in a car or enter a telephone booth.

d) **Fear of number 13:** In Western countries, some people have fear of No. 13 - 13th date, 13th floor, etc.

Fear of People

Many inventions have not progressed further just because of the fear of people. Because the inventor thinks, "What will people say?" The fear of people can instead be called 'the fear of criticism'. Many people do not speak English as they fear people's criticism if they happen to speak wrong English. A person cannot bear criticism of himself from others. If we observe our daily lives, we will find that we do or don't do many things only because of the fear of 'others'.

a) **Fear of stage:** Many people suffer from 'stage fear' or the fear of public speaking. Their thinking is that if 400 people are sitting in the audience, there are 800 eyes staring at me. What will they say if I make a mistake?

b) **Fear of teachers :** In schools, some children fear teachers or ridicule from their classmates. Due to this fear they do not attempt to ask questions. They have difficulty in even answering the questions they know well.

c) **Fear of doctors:** Many people fear doctors. Primarily some fear injections. They will take the bitterest of medicines and even tolerate health problems, but will avoid taking injections, not to speak of operations.

d) **Fear of pundits:** Pundits or priests are adept at extracting money from people by creating fear. They make statements such as, "The Gods are angry with you because you have not performed this ritual. It is very important for the well being of you and your family." Ignorant people believe in them and also fear them.

e) **Fear of boss:** People fear their boss since they fear being dismissed from their job. Owing to this fear, they are unable to work properly and constantly make mistakes.

Uncommon Fears

Comparatively fewer people have these fears:

Fear of lying: People fear that they may be caught if they tell a lie.

Fear of one's own anger: Some people fear what they may do in a fit of rage... break things, hit someone, etc.

Fear of dying unmarried: Some people fear that they may die before their marriage.

Fear of keeping a big amount: Some people fear having too much money since they believe that it may invite theft or murder.

Fear of Stars: Some people do everything after consulting the astrologers on the position of their stars. Their routine life also is at the mercy of stars.

Useful Fears

Not all fears are harmful. Some fears are necessary for our safety. E.g.: Fear of falling, fear of loud noise, fear of life threatening animals, etc. While climbing down a flight of stairs, if we start falling, we immediately catch hold of the railings. This is necessary for our body's safety. Thus, it is a useful fear.

If the fear of exam makes a student concentrate better then it is useful.

Likewise if the fear of audience makes the speaker prepare his subject matter better or if the fear of boss makes a person focused on his work, then these fears are useful.

However, if these fears increase so much that instead of helping they start hampering one's performance, then they need to be addressed.

Some Common Phobias

Agoraphobia : *an abnormal fear of being in open or public places*

Acrophobia : *an abnormal fear of being in high places*

Aerophobia : *an abnormal fear of air*

Algophobia : *an abnormal fear of pain*

Claustrophobia: *an abnormal fear of being in an enclosed or confined place*

Gynephobia : *an abnormal fear of women*

Hydrophobia : *an abnormal fear of water*

Monophobia : *an abnormal fear of being alone*

Necrophobia : *an abnormal fear of death or of dead bodies*

Zoophobia : *an abnormal fear of animals*

3 THE SIX CAUSES OF FEAR

Know the cause and eradicate the effect

There are many causes as to why fear originates. Understanding these reasons gives us an insight into eradicating fear forever.

First cause : Thoughts

Fear originates primarily from our thoughts. Our thoughts create happiness and unhappiness in our life. We can understand this through an example:

A man was lying beneath the wish fulfilling tree in paradise. Hindu mythology calls the tree as "Kalpvriksha". He wished that he could have something to eat and immediately food appeared from thin air. Next he thought he should have something to drink and a drink appeared for him. Next he wished he could have lots of wealth and he was bestowed with that. The next thought frightened him. He thought that thieves would kill him and would take away all his belongings. And the next moment he was dead.

Positive thoughts lead to positive events and negative thoughts invite negative events. Thus the first important reason for fear is our own thoughts. Our mind is our wish fulfilling tree.

Second cause : Parents

The second cause for fear to originate is the way some parents bring up their children. Parents sometimes take the support of some imaginary fears to make children do certain things such as eating a meal or going to bed. For example, a mother may tell her child, "Eat your meal quickly, otherwise ghosts will seize you and take you away." Parents don't realize that such seemingly innocent techniques do enormous damage to the child's development. Fears so created may trouble him throughout his life. Such children when they grow up suffer from various ailments and personality disorders owing to fears. At minimum, they suffer from a tremendous lack of self-confidence.

Third cause : Lack of faith in God

Lack of faith in God is also an important cause of fear. Call it the lack of faith on the universe or call it lack of knowledge of universal principles. People who do not know the principles and rules that govern the events of this world tend to be fearful of the dangerous possibilities that surround their lives. Those who know the seven principles and seven rules of nature live beyond all fears.

Fourth cause : Collective beliefs

Recently there was a rumor in one of the bordering areas of the capital that a monkey-faced man attacks people at night. It featured on TV and that further fueled the rumor. It created quite a fear in the surrounding areas and people stopped moving alone at night. Eventually it turned out to be a few unconnected mugging instances in the area, which had led to the rumor.

We tend to accept collective beliefs and fears as fact without questioning.

Many people in India still believe that – one should not keep the broom upside down... one should not sweep the house after dark... breaking of mirror is a bad omen...and so on. Some of these practices were created before the advent of electricity in our lives. Many people still observe these practices fastidiously – living a life full of ignorance, superstitions and consequent fear.

Fifth cause : Past tragic events

Some events or accidents in a person's life create fear. Some people give undue importance to a childhood event and the memory of that event becomes the basis for the related fear in their life.

For example:

Seeing someone falling in water, one starts fearing water.

After a childhood brush with dogs or seeing someone bitten by a dog, the fear of dogs remains for life. Fear of some animals like snakes, lizards, earthworms or other crawling animals is caused after seeing or hearing about them.

Fear of lizards or cockroaches because one has seen one's mother fear the same.

Fear owing to ghost stories told by grandparents.

Fears created by such events stay with us all our lives.

Sixth cause : Ordinary events of daily life

Sometimes even ordinary events of our daily routine life create fear. For example, if a child drops and breaks a glass article and the parents scold or beat the child, this could create fear in the child for such events.

A child sees his father getting upset over someone for not lifting the phone promptly. He tends to behave in the same way when he grows up. When we see people getting tensed, worried, fearful over certain things, unless we are alert, we assume this to be normal behavior and start behaving accordingly.

Food for Thought :
Thoughts are Food

What we eat is food for the body. What we see is food for eyes. Similarly thoughts are food for the mind. Whatever you are today, it is only owing to your thoughts. Whatever you think, that is the food your mind will get to chew on. Your mind will grow according to the food it gets. Man does not eat what he ought to and ends up eating what he ought not to. Man does not think what he ought to and ends up thinking what he ought not to.

FREEDOM FROM FEAR : PART ONE

Three steps that will weaken the roots of fear

First step : Face the fear and there is no fear

Do the thing you fear and the fear will disappear. If you fear going to the kitchen at night, make it a point to go there at night. The fear of going to the kitchen in the dark will disappear. Common sense says that if there is really someone in the kitchen, he can as well come to the bedroom.

If you fear your boss, find some pretext to go and speak to your boss. Gradually you will become comfortable with him.

If you fear going to stage, create situations where you have to compulsorily speak on a stage or in a group.

It takes determined efforts and courage to overcome your fears using this technique. There was a student of Tej Gyan Foundation who feared snakes. When he understood the importance of facing his fear, he took the first step of facing that fear and went to a snake park. He persuaded the officials there to allow him to have his pictures taken while holding snakes. This helped him get over his fear of snakes and increase his self-confidence.

Second step : Desensitize yourself towards the fear

The soles of our feet become tough and less sensitive compared to the rest of the skin, because of repeated contact with the ground. The same principle can be applied to overcome fears.

Do the thing you fear so often that you become insensitive to the associated fear. If you fear going to the kitchen at night, make it a point to go to the kitchen every night till you completely overcome your fear of going into dark rooms. If you fear your boss, make it a point to at least say Good Morning or Good Evening to him every day.

If you fear going on stage, then grab every opportunity to go to the stage. With each stage appearance, your fear of stage will diminish and your self-confidence will increase. Thousands of students of Tej Gyan Foundation have used this technique successfully to overcome their stage fright. Some of them eventually start enjoying the stage so much that it becomes a problem to get them off the stage.

Whatever you fear, be it open space, water, stage, darkness or your boss – face the fear repeatedly until the associated fear becomes a thing of the past.

Third step : Laugh at your fears

If you are afraid of a cockroach, think that :

"I am afraid of such a small creature. Ha! Ha!

That it will grab me. Ha! Ha! Ha!"

Laughing at your fear tends to diffuse the associated feeling of fear and makes you feel comfortable with the object of your fear. Two friends, all dressed up, were going for an interview. A bird spilled its droppings on one of them. The other friend quipped, "Oh no! What will you do now?" The first friend removed the stuff with a piece of paper, "It is nothing. Thank God, cows don't fly!" They both had a hearty laugh and walked on.

Anyone can laugh in comfortable conditions. It takes courage and wisdom to laugh in adverse conditions. We all laugh at other people's fears and mistakes. What is more important is to laugh at our own fears and mistakes.

The above three steps are equal to declaring war against fear. The next three steps are proclamation of victory.

Question in a management class

Q : Walking in a jungle, suddenly you come face to face with a tiger. What will you do?

A : I don't think I have anything to do in this scene. The tiger will do what needs to be done.

Friends of animals

'A' had gone to see a friend who had just acquired a dog. The gate had a plate that read, "Beware of Dog."

'A' shouted from the gate, "Does your dog bite?"

The friend shouted back, "Come on in. We are also waiting to find out. You are the first visitor."

5 FREEDOM FROM FEAR : PART TWO

Three steps that will make the tree of fear to fall

First step : Apply the Law of Average

Applying the Law of Average means taking an overview of factual data related to your fear. Let us see some examples:

1. A person used to fear traveling by train because of the possibility of an accident.

    What does the Law of Average say ?

    How many times do trains run between Pune and Mumbai in a year ?

    - Say about 10,000 trains.

    How many accidents take place in a year?

    - Two, three or five.

    What are the chances of an accident occurring in a train one is traveling in?

    - 5 out of 10,000. That is 0.05% .

In contrast, when a farmer ploughs his field, there is about 50% possibility of no rain, less rain or too much rain. Yet he ploughs his field. Should one then spoil his journey fearing something that has only a 0.05% possibility of occurring?

2. A student used to fear failure in exams.

   What does the Law of Average say?

   How many exams has that student taken till now?

- Say about 100.

   Though he has felt this fear of failure before each of those exams, how many times has he actually failed?

- Never. But let us suppose that he has failed once.

   What is the probability of his failing this time?

- 0% or just 1%.

If there is just a one percent possibility of failing, then why fear? As mentioned earlier, fear of exam to the extent that it helps the student concentrate better, is good. Only when it becomes too much, it needs to be tackled.

4. A woman used to fear lightning.

   What does the Law of Average say?

   How many people are there in your city?

   How many people get hit by lightning in your city every year?

   What is the percentage chance of your getting hit by lightning this year?

   It works out to be something like 0.0000001%. Why should she then live in constant fear of lightning?

In the above examples, 99% of incidents feared, usually do not occur at all. Those who use the law of average to free themselves of their fears gain courage, confidence and consequent happiness.

Second step : Rational/Logical thinking

We all have intellect, but we don't always use it. Fear in many situations can be overcome by simple use of Common Sense and Rational Thinking.

A man was going for an interview. He was mortally afraid. In this situation, let us see how he can get over his fears by using his Rational Thinking (RT).

Rational Thinking (RT) : Are you going there to beg them of something?

Interviewee (IW) : No, I am going there in response to their advertisement for a job in the newspapers.

RT : If you don't perform well, are they going to beat you up?

IW : No. They will not touch me.

RT : So, the worst that can happen is that you will not get the job you never had and you will still gain the useful experience of having attended this interview. So, what are you afraid of?

Thus, we must employ our intellect and wisdom in everyday situations to keep fear at bay.

You can use rational thinking to overcome most fears. Say, you are afraid of cockroaches. These are the common sense questions you need to ask yourself:

What harm can this small creature do to me?

Can it bite me or hurt me in any way?

Can I kill it easily if I so decide?

Who should fear whom? Should I fear the cockroach or should the cockroach fear me?

To apply rational thinking to overcome job insecurity, tell yourself that if you are doing your job wholeheartedly, nothing can happen to you. Besides getting salary, you are acquiring knowledge, experience and skills (technical, communication and others). Your boss can dismiss you from your job, but he cannot take away all of these from you.

Third step : Internal guidance - Intuition

We sometimes get a hunch that a particular person will meet me today. Our mind tells us that he is too far away to meet. Our intuition proves right and he does meet or call us.

We sometimes choose one out of many options based not on factual data but on our inner gut feeling and that choice proves to be correct. This is intuition power. We all have it.

How do birds fly away even before an impending mishap is to occur? It is intuition that guides them. In the Himalayan region, just one month before the start of snowfall, birds start flying towards the warmer regions. The most advanced of instruments fail to predict the advent of snowfall correctly. But these birds are never wrong. Who is guiding them? It is intuition. The question is do we humans have the same guiding power within us?

Intuition means tuition from within. Our Intuition is perpetually guiding us. It keeps telling us...

What is harmful for us, what is not.

Who is a friend, who is not.

Where is danger and where it is not.

...and so on.

Most of us do not cultivate this power. If we do so and also develop faith in it, it has the ability to give us correct guidance at every step. This tuition never goes wrong. Learn to listen and trust this soft voice from within.

What is important is to have faith on your intuition.

Some people watch horror shows on television and get frightened. They then fear entering a dark room thinking that there may be someone. In such cases it is necessary to tell ourselves that if there is really any danger in the room, our intuition will tell us so... provided we are listening and have learnt to trust it.

Man is so engrossed with his external (outer world) activities that he has lost touch with his intuition (inner world). This chapter is a wake up call. It is a reminder of an already existing wonderful power within us. We have to know it by experience – through listening and observation. If we do that, we realize that the source of power is within us.

Our every step is being guided from within. We have to develop faith that timely guidance comes from within when needed. Once we get tuned to our inner guidance, we will not have any fear. If at all a danger approaches us, our intuition will forewarn us.

Once in a while, do ask yourself, "What is my aim in life?" Your intuition will give you the answer. There are very few who are working towards their aim in life with full understanding and awareness. In today's fast paced life, one tends to live mechanically. One must therefore repeatedly ask oneself the above question. The answer will definitely come and this answer is of utmost importance.

'Law of Average' managed

Soon after the World Trade Center incident, a businessman was to fly his family to USA to attend his son's wedding. He was dead scared. He approached his scientist friend and asked him,

"What are the chances that someone in my plane will be carrying a bomb?" His scientist friend told, "About one in hundred."

"Oh! That's too high a chance. I can't travel. I will ask my son to postpone his wedding."

The businessman consulted his scientist friend during the successive months and every time decided to postpone his son's wedding.

Finally, on receiving an ultimatum from his son, exasperated and desperate, he consulted his friend yet again. "Have the chances improved?"

"Yes, it is now one in two hundred."

"Oh! It is still too risky. Look, what is the use of your being a scientist? You have to tell me a way to improve the chances."

Challenged, the scientist thought hard.

"There is a way." he said. The businessman looked up with hope. "You carry a bomb yourself. The chance of two persons carrying bombs in the same flight is only one in 40,000."

6 The Fear Liberating Mantra

I am God's property, no evil can touch me

The gift of courage

The fear liberating mantra is a gift of courage. It is the ace up one's sleeve to use against fear. Having applied the six steps described in the previous chapters, if one is still fearful, the sure way to be liberated from fear is by opening the gift of courage...by using the fear liberation mantra. The mantra is

"I AM GOD'S PROPERTY. NO EVIL CAN TOUCH ME."

This mantra is not just mere words. It is the power of faith based on understanding of the truth. These words have immense power and hence form a mantra. While saying this mantra, put extra emphasis on the word "touch".

By repeating these words you will feel confidence and power within you. The power of these words builds a protective wall around you. The intensity with which you pronounce these words determines the power it will generate within you. The more you repeat this mantra, the stronger your mind will become and hence negative vibrations will not get attracted towards you.

Why does this mantra have power ?

Every word carries a certain vibration. These vibrations can give you health or push you towards disease.

In ancient times people followed the path of truth. If anyone cursed or blessed someone, his or her words would come true. This was because words had the power of truth. In recent times, words are used more to mislead than to convey truth and hence the power of words is depleting. As a result we see a life full of hatred, jealousy, fears, tensions, lack of integrity and weak willpower.

Understand the power of words and use them for the benefit of yourself and others. Do the following to enhance the power of your words:

Use positive words: Instead of saying, "Don't shout!", say, "Speak softly." Instead of saying, "I have failed," say, "I have not yet succeeded."

Use inspirational words: Use words with hope in them. Words such as "I can", "I must" or "I will". Also words such as "I am fearless", "I am God's property", etc.

Do not be deceitful: Try to avoid lying as far as possible. Deceit snatches the power from our words, while truth enhances the power of our words.

Don't swear: Stop using bad, abusive words.

Use words for the benefit of others: Words of prayers, blessings, hope and growth fill the world with a new power.

Every day leave your house with some positive thoughts: Know the power of "Happy Thoughts". Keep repeating them throughout the day.

The Power of Happy Thoughts

Negative forces get attracted only to those people who are receptive to them. These people usually have a negative approach to things and are afraid within. Fearful and unhappy people tend to withdraw and have space within for negative forces to occupy. Fearless and happy people tend to expand keeping all the space filled with positive forces.

A fearful person is porous like a sponge. In a sponge, the water gets absorbed due to holes present in it. Don't make yourself porous. Every time you feel scared, just repeat the mantra and all the pores in your body will get filled, leaving no space for fear.

Excerpt from a Seeker's conversation with Sirshree

Seeker   : *Sirshree, I fear doctors.*

Sirshree : *Is it actually the fear of injection?*

Seeker   : *No.*

Sirshree : *Then, why do you fear?*

Seeker   : *I fear his bill. Do you have a cure for that?*

Sirshree : *Avoid falling sick.*

Seeker   : *How?*

Sirshree : *Stop eating for doctors.*

Seeker   : *Please explain.*

Sirshree : *Every time you overeat or eat when not hungry, you are eating for doctors. Use your fear of giving away your wealth to doctors by reminding yourself of this fear whenever you overeat.*

Seeker   : *Oh. This is wonderful. I thought I should get rid of fears. Now I see something new...using the fear. Anything else I should do?*

Sirshree : *Drink plenty of water, exercise regularly, and most importantly – keep HAPPY THOUGHTS.*

7 LIBERATION FROM THE FEAR OF DEATH
How to kill the fear of death

Everyone seems to fear death. In fact, fear of death is the root of all the different fears that people have - be it the fear of darkness, the fear of animals, the fear of future or the fear of old age.

Nature has given us the fear of death for a specific reason. Understand this through an analogy. Suppose a school gate has a beautiful picture on its outer side and a frightening picture on its inner side. While entering the school gate, the child will see the beautiful picture. Once he has entered, if he ever tries to run away from school before he has learnt his lessons, he will see the frightening picture and this will make him run back towards the school instead of towards the gate. Thus he will spend his entire lifetime in the school and will never approach the gate (contemplate suicide). This is why the fear of death has been instilled in our minds.

Without this fear, the number of suicides would have increased manifold. Many would have left the earth without fulfilling the purpose of their birth. However, those who have acquired the necessary maturity must outgrow this fear too.

The main reason behind the fear of death is incomplete knowledge. At some point or the other, you must have heard the following:

Once you die, what was dust goes back to dust.

Death is the only truth.

Death is the biggest illusion.

The soul never dies.

Death is a forecast that never proves wrong.

Owing to such beliefs, the concept of death has remained a mystery. The lack of knowledge about death makes death appear frightening. If we truly understand what death is, then death itself can teach us the art of living. To live life well, one must understand death.

When we fall asleep, we lose all awareness of the body. We actually go through a mini-death. However, we are not afraid of falling asleep because we understand sleep. Once we understand death, we will stop fearing death too.

Sleep is a short death that happens every day. Death is a long sleep that happens once.

What we call death is actually a stage in life. Just as childhood, adolescence, adulthood, middle age and old age are various stages of life, death is also a phase.

Our body has five layers. When we die, only the outer two layers are shed. The inner three layers (astral body and other bodies) remain. The astral body is not visible to the naked eye and hence we declare the person dead. But in reality, the death of our body is not our death but the beginning of life after life.

The astral body continues its onward journey and after a long period the astral body dies too. This should be considered as true death. Since these facts are beyond the comprehension of our mind and senses, we fear death.

A warning

By reading the above facts that have been explained just briefly in this book, one should not contemplate suicide so that the astral body can be experienced. Incomplete understanding is very harmful. As essential as understanding death is, more essential is to understand the purpose of human birth. Until we have learnt all that we are to learn in this physical form, trying to go prematurely to the astral form is wrong and harmful. The understanding of truth acquired while in the physical body proves most helpful in the onward journey of the astral body. We must understand that the wisdom acquired here continues with us in the life after death. The bliss achieved here is multiplied manifold in our onward life after death. (You can read in detail about life after death in the book titled 'Life After Death' published by Tej Gyan Foundation).

The purpose of telling the above is to drive away the fear of death. Death is a natural, necessary event in the evolution of each individual. It should neither be feared nor embraced prematurely. Some normal fear of physical injury is natural and is necessary for our safety.

What has been said above is only an indication. Do not conclude this as the whole truth about life. Only on understanding the Bright Truth (Tejgyan), can you be liberated in the true sense.

Question in a management class

Boss   : *Do you believe in life after death?*

Employee : *Why Sir?*

Boss   : *While you were away yesterday afternoon to attend your grandmother's funeral, she dropped in to see you.*

8 The Instant Way to be Rid of Fear

The power of imagination

What you have read so far can be used to combat any kind of fear. You will have to face some fears to be rid of them. You will have to use logic to combat some. You will use the mantra against some fears. However, there may be certain extraordinary fears which are deep rooted in your subconscious mind. Use the technique outlined below for such fears. Even if your fear is deep rooted to the extent that a cockroach seems to appear like a dinosaur to you, this technique will instantly get you rid of your fear.

The Third Camera Technique

Take a deep breath. Slowly exhale. Close your eyes. And imagine that...

1. You are standing atop the balcony of the third floor of a house. Or you are poised at one corner of the ceiling (roof) in an empty room. (This is called looking tall).

2. From the top, see a second image of yourself. See the second image of yourself with a stick in your hand.

3. See yourself fearing the object of your fear. It could be an insect, an animal, etc.

4. From the top, see the object of your fear on the ground in front of your second image. Eg : If you fear an insect, see the insect in front of you.

5. See yourself (the second image) pushing away the insect with the stick.

6. See the insect approaching you once more. Once more push it away with the stick.

7. See this repeatedly. Remember you are only seeing this from quite far...from atop the ceiling or from top of the balcony.

8. You are enjoying pushing away the insect so much that you are doing it repeatedly.

9. Now see yourself pushing away the insect and simultaneously hear the band of a circus playing in the background. You are now pushing away the insect on the beats of the music. This might seem quite funny.

10. See yourself from top and afar standing down, pushing away the insect repeatedly as you listen to the band playing in the background.

11. Once you are able to see the complete picture with music clearly, now see the same picture in quick motion in the reverse order repeatedly, as if you have pushed the rewind button in your mind.

12. Now see the same picture rapidly in the forward order as if you have pushed the 'fast forward' button in your mind. The speed of things occurring should go up significantly and so also the pace of music.

13. Having seen it in the reverse and forward direction, see it happening in slow motion.
14. Ask yourself how do you feel now. Is the fear still unpleasant?
15. Repeat the visualization technique two more times.
16. Slowly open your eyes.

You may repeat this visualization technique after a few days.

You can use this technique for any type of fear. You may even use it for stage fear. Instead of the insect, see an audience. Instead of pushing the insect away with a stick, see yourself speaking to the audience comfortably. The whole idea behind this technique is to get a second image of yourself facing the fear. Since it is a second image and you are anyway standing afar, the fear is not as frightening.

In this technique, you also end up dislodging the pattern of that fear stored in your nervous system. You now record a different picture in your subconscious mind. As you use the technique, the fear that seemed so dangerous once becomes something quite funny. The emotion underlying the fear vanishes.

Use this technique for curing yourself of any unnecessary fears.

World's Greatest Psychiatrist

There is one very good psychiatrist who can rid you of all your fears. Take down his name and address.

Name : ....
..

(write your name here)

Address : ....
..

(write your address here)

Yes, you are the psychiatrist who will drive away all your fears. Others can guide you, give you a book, cassette, etc., but finally you have to ACT and win over your fears.

The Ultimate Way to Be Rid of Fear

Take an oath that you will not die before your death

One of the main causes of fear is ignorance. Call it 'lack of wisdom' or 'incomplete knowledge'. In the absence of proper knowledge, people fear a lot of things and die many times - some of them a thousand deaths every day - before the actual death of their body.

If you have to visit the doctor in the evening for taking an injection, then do you dread that from morning itself? The pain of injection will occur only in the evening. But you feel the pain many times from morning onwards, even before the incident has occurred. This is due to ignorance.

Ignorance or half knowledge is dangerous. Half knowledge is usually inculcated in the early days of childhood. Parents think that they should inform their children of all the untoward events that come with life. To educate their children about reality, parents tell children about planes being hijacked, trains falling off rails, epidemics spreading, etc. It is true that children need to be educated about reality. But avoid giving half knowledge. Give them the whole picture.

Half Knowledge

Parents tell the truths of life to their children. But what truths? Usually those truths that they have experienced, those problems that they have suffered. They tell their children with the fear that their children should not undergo the same bitter or fearful experiences they went through. But parents don't know that they are only painting a part of the picture. They are breeding ignorance by imparting half knowledge.

Complete Knowledge

Tell your children that planes may be hijacked, trains may fall off rails, epidemics may spread, but…"Die only once in life. The courageous die only once." Once they know this fact, they do not die again and again. If you do not tell your children of this very important step, then you are giving them partial knowledge.

So let us make a promise today -

I will not die again and again.

I will not die before my death.

I will die only once whenever it happens on its own.

A Tall Summary of Book One

Walk Tall:

Face the fear and there is no fear. (Chapter 4)

Talk Tall:

I am God's property, no evil can touch me. (Chapter 6)

Laugh Tall:

Laugh at your fears. (Chapter 4)

Think Tall:

Use rational thinking and the law of average. (Chapter 5)

Look Tall:

See great to be great. Look tall from top of the roof and witness yourself. (Chapter 8)

Oath Tall:

Die once. Never die before your death. (Chapter 7, 9)

Self Liberation
Book Two : Worry

WHAT IS WORRY

Understanding worry, anxiety, stress and panic

What is worry?

Worry is a general sense of uneasiness or distress. It is the vague feeling that causes one to be insecure and unsure. Also known as apprehension, alarm and anxiety, it describes an emotional state of expecting possible unpleasant events.

Man worries because he lacks knowledge of the future and fears his limited capacity. Mothers worry whether their children will be safe, responsible, well settled. Children worry whether they are living up to their parents' expectations. Students worry whether they will pass their exams. Lawyers worry whether they have made persuasive arguments. Doctors worry whether they have made the correct diagnosis and if their patients will be cured. Patients worry whether the treatment will be effective and they will regain their health. The list of people worrying about themselves and others is endless.

The effects of worry

There are many negative consequences of worry.

Some of them are mentioned below :

    Failing health

    Disturbed sleep

    Not liking food

    Not liking humor or small talk

    Irritation over minor things

    Stressful behavior

    Diminishing discriminative power

    Feeling of being lost

Stress

Stress is described as a state of worry which results from pressure caused by problems of living, too much work, etc. Stress is a common scenario at work. Although it may be hard to define what exactly stress is, it is perhaps true to say all of us have experienced it and are still experiencing it. The word stress was borrowed from physics in which it refers to the application of a physical force upon an object. When deformity occurs as a result, it is called strain. Thus when we refer to the stresses and strains of living, we mean anything and everything that challenges our comfort in life.

Knowing the difference

Worry and Fear: Worry differs from fear in that there is no specific object or situation that is feared. Rather, it is the vague feeling of uneasiness and of being uncomfortable. Magnified worry takes the form of fear. Magnified fear takes the form of phobia. The relationship between fear and worry is that fear leads to worry and worry leads to fear. It is a vicious cycle.

Worry and Stress: Unlike stress, which has to do with our reaction to external stimulus, worry has to do with trying to keep the lid on what is stirred up inside us. Many of us live all the time expecting disapproval. We do not understand why. We question our place in the world in which we live. We are sure we are not quite good enough.

Worry and Panic: Worry should also not be confused with panic. Panic shuts us down. It is debilitating. It renders us ineffective and unresponsive. Worry does not do so.

Worry and Anxiety: Anxiety is a state of being uneasy, apprehensive, or worried about what may happen; concern about a possible future event. Simply stated, there is no difference between 'Worry' and 'Anxiety'. It is a matter of choice of words.

Which answer do you like?

Answer One : Learn to fight (and conquer) worry.

Answer Two : First stop worrying about worry.

Answer Three : Make worry a ladder for your success.

Answer Four : Magnify your worry so much that you have to now worry about the whole world.

From the answers above – which answer did you like? What you liked tells about the state of your mind. If you did not like any of the answers, then this book is not for you.

If you liked the first answer – then you will obtain courage from this book.

If you liked the second answer – then you will explore the depths of worry and then become liberated from it.

If you liked the third answer – then you are ready to be liberated from worry.

If you liked the fourth answer – then you will be inspired to attain the "Bright Truth" (Tejgyan) from this book.

The Invisible Way to be Rid of Worry

Prayer – The greatest power

A powerful way to be liberated from worry is through prayer. Prayer is a state of being where man experiences the grace of the Almighty. Prayer is a way of conversing with God.

The universe contains various kinds of people and also contains various objects. The moment a need is created in one man, the object to fulfill the need automatically begins to be drawn towards him. Prayer creates the platform by which what we want begins to manifest in our life. Prayer is the answer to the question, "How to get what you want?" Birth of man is in itself a prayer. The desire of a seeker to know the truth is prayer. Man begins to pray when he seeks the truth. Man begins to pray when he wants a cure for his miseries. When man is unhappy or he sees someone else unhappy, he seeks a way out of this unhappiness. He yearns for some power that will get him rid of all unhappiness.

Such a thought, such state of seeking is a form of prayer. One day he cries out to be freed from his misery. Then he experiences that some events occur in his life such that his problems are solved and he is alleviated from his misery. That heartfelt cry is prayer too.

We need to understand how prayer works. Prayer works because of a law of the universe. The law of the universe is that every problem is pregnant with its own solution. Before a problem arises in life, the solution to that problem is already given to you. Remember this whenever worry torments you. Remember that whenever a problem arises, you have already been bestowed with its solution. The universe provides for a child's milk even before the child is born. Thus every problem contains its own solution. The only thing to be done is to find the pre-provided solution, which is within you. Prayer helps you find that solution.

Prayer is the greatest power of the universe. It is a power given to man even before his problems arise. It is but foolish not to use this great power and remain in an ego trap. As you continue to use the power of prayer, you will experience how it becomes a medium of conversing with God.

The power of prayer is immense. Prayer can move mountains, can extinguish raging fires, can control furious storms, can save sinking boats and can produce miracles. Prayer fulfills desires. Prayer can even lead to liberation. Prayer is equal to handing over your worries to a higher source. Pray and hand over your fears and worries to God and be convinced that He will handle it appropriately. This technique will attract every possible solution to your problem.

Pray to the one who is ahead of you, even if slightly. Pray to the one who is higher than you. Pray to the Ultimate. By praying, the possibility of reaching those heights increases. Pray to only the one whom you consider to be great. You could pray to God,

Guru, Universe, God at Rest, Self... Pray to someone or something you have faith on and know the greatness of whom you are praying to and have faith that this prayer will work.

The World's Greatest Prayer

A village simpleton used to pray to God every day. He used to pray using a book of prayers. Never came a day that he did not pray. Once he had to visit the city. When it was time for him to pray, he realized that he did not have his book of prayers. He prayed thus: "God, I don't have words to pray. I will chant A, B, C,...Z. Please make up the words using these alphabets." On hearing this, God said to his angels, "This is the greatest prayer I have heard so far."

The moral of this story is that in prayer words do not matter. It is the feeling and the intensity with which you say the prayer that matters.

3 · The In-depth Way to be Rid of Worry

Stop worrying about worry

Worrying about worry is real worry. Otherwise worry is no worry at all. Man is troubled because of what is called as double worry. Say you are troubled over something. And you are also troubled over being troubled. This is what is termed as double worry. Another example could be when the body is in pain. When the body is in pain, the mind is pained over the pain and raises questions such as, "Why do I have pain?" "Why me?" "When will I be relieved of this pain?" etc. Such pain over pain is multifold pain. The body was in pain. The body was being treated. The body is capable of handling and curing the pain. Nature has endowed the body with curative powers. But the mind made the pain as "my" pain and multiplied the pain manifold.

Look at a child in anger. It is angry one moment and playful the next. But when you are in anger, you tend to create 'anger' over anger - "Oh, why do I get so angry?" "I shouldn't get angry." "I should have controlled it." "I am frustrated at my lack of self-control." Even after the bout of anger is over, you tend to think about it for hours together. This is precisely the problem. Thus anger over anger or worry about worry distresses the mind. The more you understand this, the more easily you will be able to get rid of double worry.

Understand that worry has been given to you to get some work done from you. You worry about your forthcoming exams - you study. Thus worry is a guidepost for your future. Learn to grab at the opportunity of being worried. Take appropriate action. Then worrying about worry, fearing fear, tension on tension ceases.

Going forward, whenever you are tensed or worried over something, remember these five steps:

1. Accept your tension or worry first.
2. There is no need to be more tensed about being tensed. 'Tension on tension' is the result of ignorance.
3. When there is no tension on tension, getting off tension is fairly simple.
4. Repeat to yourself that now that this tension or worry has arisen, there is something I need to act upon. This action ultimately leads to my growth.
5. Whenever there is tension, it would have left you with a lesson – a lesson of understanding. A lesson that would have taught you the art of being peaceful even while in tension.

Not only can you use the five steps mentioned above for worry or tension, but also for anger and fear.

You eat yesterday's food today

When you go to a restaurant, you do not eat the food actually of the day you have visited the restaurant. It is not that the food is stale. It means that when you visit a restaurant, you think about how good the food was the last time you visited some other restaurant. Thus in your mind, you are eating the food of that other restaurant from your past. Tomorrow when you go to another restaurant, you will actually eat the food that you are eating today.

When you eat, just eat. When you worry, just worry. There is no need to worry about worry, to worry about how you had no worries in the past, or to worry about how you will worry in the future.

THE FIRST WAY TO BE RID OF WORRY

The one hour worry cure technique

Man fasts a lot. He goes without food for the sake of his health or out of fear of God. Man thinks a lot about the food he feeds himself... whether he should eat something or not... the impact of what he is eating... whether he will enjoy it or not... Obviously it is important to think so, because certain foods have a negative impact on the body. But such thinking is secondary. What then is primary?

What is primary is what you are feeding your mind with. Have you ever reflected on what thoughts you feed your mind in twenty-four hours? Are you feeding positive thoughts or negative thoughts? These are thoughts that affect your whole life. You have always used only two ways to combat worry – fight or flight. A better way is to face it.

Face the worry by acknowledging it and by just being with it without worrying over worry. Face the worry by deciding a fixed amount of time where you will not worry at all, come what may. This is what is called as WORRY FAST. To start with, decide an hour of the day where you will be on a worry fast. During that hour you will not entertain any thoughts of worry at all. You are welcome to worry later as much as you want. During that one hour, whatever incident happens, however terrible it may seem, carry through your resolve of not getting worried. During that hour, someone might inform you that belongings have been stolen. Retort back saying that you will not worry since it is none of your business. That person will emphasize that it is YOUR belongings that have been stolen. Retort back saying that then he need not worry since it is none of his business. This example emphasizes that during your hour of worry fast, no incident should affect you however adverse it is.

Choose an hour out of your schedule as per your convenience. There already might be a time of the day where you are most stressed. Some are stressed in the morning since they hurry a lot. That is the perfect time then to go on a worry fast. Some may be most anxious at work. Then accordingly choose an hour at work. There are many who are disturbed when they are back home from work. They try to calm their disturbed mind by diverting the mind elsewhere, by watching television, consuming alcohol, gambling, gossiping, etc. The result is that they invite more worry unnecessarily. Instead of a 'flight' from worry, face it. Face it by going on a worry fast. One hour of worry fast strengthens your ability to face worry. This hour is a great investment.

The procedure of worry fast is very simple. Staunchly determine to abstain from worry during that hour. Tell yourself that you will remain cool, calm and composed for the next one hour. Then during that hour, when an event that triggers worry occurs, remind yourself that you are on a worry fast. Begin practising with one hour. Once you have tasted being worry free, even for an hour, then the process of being liberated from worry is set in motion.

Things to do every day

Worry fast is something that you should attempt every day. Being on a worry fast requires willpower. You can take up more tasks every day consciously similar to a worry fast to increase your willpower:

1. *Consciously do one or two things against your will every day – things that you don't like to do or things that you usually postpone.*

2. *Every night before you go to sleep, ask yourself, "Is there any other task that I can complete right now?" Then go ahead and complete that task.*

3. *Cultivate the habit of learning something new every day. The learning habit pulls you out of mental inertia and physical laziness.*

4. *Cultivate the habit of writing a diary or journal. Write your things to do, write about your willpower exercises, your worry fast, results of techniques for worry and fear cure that you have learnt from this book, etc. Write about all the self-development work you are doing. Writing a diary is a powerful self-growth tool. If required, involve a friend who will review your diary and remind, motivate or guide you from time to time.*

5 The Second Way to be Rid of Worry

Desensitize yourself from worry

What you have learned so far is that instead of 'fight or flight', face worry. When you practice facing worry continuously, you desensitize yourself from worry. You can start facing worry by being on a worry fast for one hour in a day as explained in the previous chapter. Gradually increase your worry fast to twice a day for an hour each.

Remember you are on a war against worry. Every hour is a battle. Win every battle and you win the war. Proceed to be on a worry fast for one-and-a-half hours twice a day every day. Gradually continue to increase the time limit. Increase it from one to two… to three… to four… until you are firmly convinced that whatever may be the incident, you will not be worried. Until you can confidently face worry. Until you can be worriless the whole day. Until you are completely desensitized from worry.

To be desensitized from anything, you need to carry out that activity several times, not just once. To site the same example again, the soles of your feet or the palms of your hands are desensitized. Once upon a time, they were very sensitive. But through repeated use on the floor, over stones, on rocks – they have become very strong. This is the same principle you need to apply against worry. Then facing worry becomes a game.

Desensitize your way to self-confidence

The easiest way to self-confidence is by desensitizing yourself against whatever you are not confident about. If you are not a confident public speaker, find all the opportunities you can to speak on stage. The more you speak, the more you are desensitized from stage fear and the more your confidence improves. Train yourself to accept challenges. If you are not confident about meeting people, then challenge your fear and go and talk to someone who is unknown. The key is to do this every day. Initially, the mind will find this uncomfortable. But that is the whole point. Challenging yourself and desensitizing yourself from what you are not confident about will magnify your confidence by leaps and bounds.

6. The Third Way to Be Rid of Worry

Three questions, three steps, one formula

Three Questions to annihilate worry

Whenever you are worried, do ask yourself the following three questions. Through these questions, the truth about worry will be revealed to you.

First Question : Whatever things I have worried would occur, have they really occurred?

Answer : No. Only a few events out of those might have occurred.

Second Question : Whatever did occur, was it as dreadful as I had imagined it to be?

Answer : No. Out of the few that did occur, only a handful were really dreadful.

Third Question : However dreadful those countable few events turned out to be, were you able to face them?

Answer : Definitely, I could face them.

Conclusion : If you have faced such events in the past, won't you be able to face such events even in the future? Then why is there a need to sit and brood over the future and generate worry? First of all, whatever you think will occur… won't occur. Even if it did, it will not be as dreadful as you think it would be. Even if it were dreadful, then you do have a history of facing such events successfully. Thus you will be able to face them even in the future. All you need to do is some honest enquiry with yourself. Such enquiry will reveal the futility of playing the tape of worry in your mind over and over. You will realize that you have the habit of rewinding the tape and playing it again and again. Through self-enquiry, an awareness will arise that will keep you out of worrying even in the most dreadful of situations.

Three Steps – One Formula

First Step: Whenever you worry, ask yourself what is the worst that might happen? What at the most?

Explanation: Thinking so prepares you for the worst, whether your worst fears come true or not. Whatever you think might be the worst, usually does not happen at all. The probability is barely 5- 10%.

Second Step: Accept what is the worst that can happen.

Explanation: First conjure up what is the worst that can happen. Then accept the worst. If you accept something, then it cannot torment you. Inability to accept leads to unhappiness.

Third Step : Take action in whatever time is left

Explanation: Without the third step, this formula is incomplete. Complete the formula by taking the third step. You know what is the worst that could happen. So, in whatever time is left, take corrective action. Do what you can to prevent further loss. This is similar to darning your clothes. You know your shirt is torn and you cannot bring back the original condition of your shirt. So you go to a darner and mend as much as you can.

This formula of imagining what is the worst that could happen, then accepting it and then taking action is a powerful one. By applying this three-step formula, you will find that ninety-nine out of hundred times, whatever you feared as the worst, does not occur at all.

Fear of Failure

The three-step technique explained in the previous topic to combat worry is especially useful to tackle the fear of failure. A student might fear failing in his examination. There are many students who have barely any time left for studying and who while away the remaining time worrying over their fate. If a student knows this formula, he would first imagine what is the worst that could happen. At worst he might fail. He then accepts that he might fail. He accepts the consequence of it. This brings immediate relief to him. Finally in whatever little time is left, he makes amends. Now the fear of failure no longer paralyses him or keeps him from studying. This gives him confidence and he gets down to work. And in the end, he finds that whatever he had feared, that never even occurred. This technique could be used for any performance related fear or anxiety.

The Practical Way to Be Rid of Worry

The law of average wrecks worry and destroys delusion

Parents frequently worry about their children. They have the delusion that unless they worry about their children, they are not being responsible parents. They think that if they don't worry, they are not doing their duty. What they don't know is that such negative thoughts may even harm their child. What parents should be doing is to be practical and apply the law of average. The law of average is not just applicable to parents when they worry about their children, it is applicable to most worries.

The law of average operates on a simple premise: "Worry is very much unreal since it is just in a thought form. What is real is the truth. The truth is very much real." To apply the law of average, ask yourself, "What does reality say? What do facts say?" The application of this law may seem difficult. In reality, it is the simplest and most practical. Let us understand the law of average through an example.

Understanding The Law of Average

A mother is constantly worried about her child that he would be injured in an accident. She is plagued by these thoughts without any reason.

All she has to do is to ask herself the facts applying the law of average:

Q. On an average, how many times has my son stepped out of the house?

A. Around 4000 times. (Assuming that the son is 15 years old and he has been going out since the age of 5. Assuming further that in ten years be might have gone out at least once a day).

Q. In the past 15 years, how many times has he been hurt?

A. Around 4 times.

Q. So what is the probability of he getting hurt today?

A. It works out to 4/4000, which is a 0.001% probability of getting hurt.

Q. Is there any reason that I should then worry if the odds are 1:1000?

A. Definitely no.

That is how you can apply the law of average. If you are worried about going bankrupt, find the average number of people going bankrupt. It is usually a negligible amount. Never more than a 1% possibility. In that case, why worry about something that might not even occur?

Some calculations about life

Q. What is the biggest thing in the world?

A. The sky.

Q. What is the fastest thing in the world?

A. Thought.

Q. What is given out in the most quantity?

A. Advice.

Q. What is the most difficult thing in the world?

A. To know yourself.

Q. What is the easiest thing in the world?

A. To know yourself.

Q. What is the way to liberation from worry?

A. To know yourself. Any other question?

Q. (Seeker): No. I now know what the answer will be. Know yourself... know yourself... know yourself.

The Illogical Way to Be Rid of Worry
Learn To Laugh At Your Worries

When things are going fine, everyone can laugh. It is no big deal. But it takes courage to laugh in the face of adversity. If you can laugh at your pain, then it soothes your pain. Very few people can laugh at their worries.

You can laugh at your worries by looking at its futility, probability or your own stupidity to blow up things. Laughing at yourself, especially when there is tension among relationships, lightens up the situation immediately. It is a habit you need to develop to see the funny side of things.

Q. What will you do if someone who is drinking water mistakenly spills some drops on your written work?

A. You can quip back saying that it is good that you don't drink ink.

All you need to do is to see the lighter side of things and comment upon it.

Determine staunchly that whenever you are worried, you will laugh at your worries. Laughing at your mistakes and follies is the best medicine for you.

The Power of Truth

Once a widow's only son drowned in the village pond. The widow was devastated. The entire village gathered around her son's drowned body. A saint happened to be camping near the village. Someone suggested that they should go to the saint. All the villagers went down to the saint's hut carrying the body with them.

The widow fell on the saint's feet and cried out, "Sir, I will not be able to live without my son. Please help me. Please get me my son back." The saint closed his eyes and sat in silence for a while. Then he opened his eyes and spoke softly, "Dearest, I just prayed for guidance. I am told that if each one of us gathered here speaks words of truth, casting away some prevailing false in our life, the collective power of our words of truth can give life to your son."

Suddenly every one became still. The rays of the setting sun illuminated their faces. Each one was feeling the sanctity of the developing situation. The saint was the first to speak, "Though I am fortunate enough to be pure in my outward deeds so far, I have committed many wrongs in my thoughts. May God help me to be as pure in thoughts too." The confectioner spoke next, "I have been cheating you all ever since by using lesser weights." The Pundit said, "I am no messenger of God. I have been routinely telling people lies that make them donate more to me." The moneylender admitted to having fudged records of some deceased persons to cheat their survivors. Some confessed of theft, others of having told lies in specific important situations and so on.

By the time they had all finished, it was midnight. The moon was shining bright over them. They were all totally silent – eyes closed, experiencing thoughtless purity of heart. No one even noticed when the 'drowned' boy rolled over into his mother's lap. They quietly dispersed after greeting the rising sun.

The life in that village became perpetually joyous ever since. The people there had learnt to live by the truth.

9 The Intelligent Way to be Rid of Worry

The power of rational thinking

Man has been bestowed with intellect. But there are very few who use their intellect to maximum benefit. The question is not how much you use your intellect, the question is whether you use it at the right time, right place and the right way (rationally). That is why it is said that common sense is uncommon. Use of common sense or rational thinking is one of the easiest ways to be rid of worry. Just by thinking rationally on the outcome and the impact of a troublesome event, you can kill worry.

Once a businessman heard that something negative about him has been printed in the 'Times of India', a national daily. He got extremely worried about whether he will be able to face society. He even contemplated suicide. All he needs to do is to use rational thinking.

What Does Rational Thinking Have To Say?

Rational Thinking (RT) : How many people read the 'Times of India' in your city?

Individual (IN) : About a hundred thousand (one lakh) read the Times of India.

RT : How many actually would read the whole newspaper?

IN : Around 50,000.

RT : Out of those 50,000, how many would have registered what they read?

IN : Around 25,000.

RT : Out of 25,000, how many would know you by name?

IN : May be around 5000.

RT : Out of them, how many can associate you by name and face, i.e. how many know you personally?

IN : Probably 500.

RT : Out of these 500 how many would have read it and continue to remember it after a week?

IN : Probably 250.

RT : Out of those 250, how many would have believed the news about you?

IN : Maybe 50.

RT : Out of the 50, how many people knowing it will impact you personally or professionally?

IN : Around 10.

RT : Out of these 10, how many will clarify with you as to whether the news is correct?

IN : Almost all will clarify. Now I understand how foolish I was to worry about it.

RT : Yes. And by the way, we did not consider the advantages that negative publicity has too. It is a great marketing tool.

Thus if you rationally think about what are your worries, most of your worries will vanish.

Rationally examine your 'musts'.

*Most worries related to performance and people is because of a predominant belief – "I **must** perform well and get approval from others or else I am useless." If you worry about your performance, rationally examine this belief. Ask yourself : "Is it really a must?" "How is it true?" "Is it written somewhere?" Once you are convinced that it is a mere belief without any foundation, you will see that your 'must' is entirely false. Change your belief to, "I like to perform well" or "I prefer to perform well" instead of clinging to "must". Rationally check your other worries too. Is there a 'must' underlying those worries? Rationally examine that belief and let it go. Your worries will also go.*

10 THE KNOWLEDGEABLE WAY TO BE RID OF WORRY

Know the irrefutable law of life

One of the irrefutable laws of life is: "Everything is constantly changing." Everything other than this law is changing. Knowing this law gives you courage when sorrow follows happiness and saves you from being too excited when happiness follows sorrow (and thus does not fuel the ego).

The moment there is change in life we become worried. Instead of finding the reason behind the change, we tend to blame others. There are four areas of change in life due to which one worries. Know how these areas of change can become the cause of worry and unhappiness:

Changes in profession (work)

The moment you are out of college, you find something to do. Either you work for someone or work for yourself (business or self employed profession). A day comes when everything is going smoothly. You are very much settled. Suddenly there is a change. You are either transferred to another department, posted to another city or given additional responsibilities or maybe even sacked from your job. There is change in what you were doing comfortably so far. If you are running a business, cyclical changes affect you and what follows is worry. The same business or profession that once used to bring immense joy is now a cause of immense worry.

Another example could be that of recession in the economy. Factories closing down, businesses being shut down, workers being laid off are some of the consequences of recession. In such a scenario, every employee constantly worries about whether he will be sacked from his job. Every employer is worried about keeping his business afloat. Not only do employees and businessmen worry, they pass on their worries to their wives and children. They pass their worries on to their friends who in turn now start worrying about their jobs. Their wives and children start worrying... In this way the whole society, the whole nation gets permeated with worry and negative thoughts.

Changes in individuals

The second area is change in individuals. This encompasses changes in relatives, changes in friends, etc. Your friends or relatives may change. They may leave you. They may be transferred to another city or they may even die. Some people cannot bear such changes. Some are completely unable to cope up with such changes to the extent that they become mental wrecks.

There are others who see someone near and dear change their behaviour. They hate the change. Lifelong they bear a grudge because of the change in behaviour. Thus, refusal to accept change leads to resentment. Just because the law of change has not been understood, resentful individuals suffer a lot. The consequence is that a self-created aura of unhappiness, fear, hatred, melancholy and anger constantly surrounds such individuals. All these are second cousins of worry and invite worry to join the party.

Changes in the environment

Changes in the environment may lead to health changes or lifestyle changes. Some cannot adapt to these changes. They lament about their sickness. They convince themselves with a lie that someone else is responsible for the change. They feel secure temporarily because of this lie. What they don't realize is that this self-deception ultimately leads to worry.

Changes in objects

Objects change. Some individuals are very much attached to objects. They always fear that the object of their attachment may break, may get spoilt, may get lost or may get stolen. But things change. That is the law of change. Such individuals worry about this inevitable change.

Change your understanding and keep the change

To tackle all the above four areas of change, all you have to do is to understand the law of change: "Everything changes other than change." Understand that when something changes, you get something new – new friends, new relations, new jobs, new businesses, new things... If you truly understand this, then change becomes something to celebrate than to worry about. You will thank change since something new has been created in your life.

The main cause of worry during change is that people pass a judgment about the change. They conjure up images about the consequences of change. It is best to avoid judgment or imagination before the change transpires. When you look at change with patience and courage, all that you had conjured up proves to be wrong. Collect all the information you can before conjuring up something or deciding to do something about the change. Once all the information has been gathered and you see the complete picture, then every change will be acceptable and the change will turn out to be just right for you.

If you have understood the law of change, then you will always be prepared for change. You will constantly strive to seek newer avenues in life. You will see change as something very beautiful and something you are already prepared for.

When A Glass Breaks

When a glass of milk falls down and breaks and there are glass pieces on the floor, there are ways to react...

Some ask, "Who kept the glass on the table?"

Some ask, "What was the cost of the milk that was wasted?"

Some ask, "Why are you always so careless?"

What is more important is to ask, "What is to be done next?" What is needed is to only remove the glass pieces from the floor. That is all. Crying over spilt milk is merely another form of worry. Remove the glass and remove your worry.

11 The Positive Way to be Rid of Worry

Your attitude determines your altitude

If you worry about something, you think negatively. Instead if you contemplate about something, you think positively. Change your viewpoint about worry. Adopt the viewpoint of contemplation. Your attitude determines how you face failure. A positive thinker takes every failure as a stepping-stone. He converts his failures into successes. Such people are welcomed wherever they go. It is such positive thinkers who inspire people, who cultivate a feeling of brotherhood wherever they go and help in creating a stress free society. The difference between negative thinking and positive thinking is highlighted in the following examples:

Worry (Negative Thinking) says: What if I don't get anything inspite of hardwork?

Contemplation (Positive Thinking) says: Even if my hardwork doesn't pay off, at least I will grow stronger physically and mentally. And there is no harm in trying.

Worry : Will I be as happy tomorrow as I am today?

Contemplation	:	There must be ways and means to attain permanent happiness, which I need to seek.
Worry	:	There are many cracks (worries) in the mirror of life.
Contemplation	:	So what if there are cracks in the mirror of life? The mirror still reflects my face.
Worry	:	Things can get worse.
Contemplation	:	Things can only get better. The possibility of happiness is immense. Happiness is my second nature.
Worry	:	Everything nowadays is unhealthy... the environment, the water, the food, the air.
Contemplation	:	Actually bad conditions increase the resistance of my body. And even if I do fall sick, I will only come out stronger.
Worry	:	Trains can get derailed, cars may collide, planes may be hijacked.
Contemplation	:	What is the probability of these things occurring? What does the law of average say?
Worry	:	In everything I undertake, there is risk. One should avoid risks.
Contemplation	:	One should take calculated risks. That is the only way to progress.
Worry	:	What is the bad news today? Where is trouble brewing? Any riots? Any wars? Any murders?
Contemplation	:	What are the new developments today? Any new discoveries? What challenges do the events of the world pose to me?
Worry	:	How will my decision turn out to be? I do not

	have any experience. It is best that I do not take any decisions at all.
Contemplation :	Instead of not deciding at all, it is better to make wrong decisions and learn from wrong decisions. Good decisions come from experience and experience comes from bad (wrong) decisions.
Worry :	Why do bad things happen to good people?
Contemplation :	Whatever happens, I am equipped with the solution before the problem itself.
Worry :	I am worried about death.
Contemplation :	My worry is dying.

Worrying about sun signs

There are many who read every day what their sun signs say in the newspapers and get worried about the same. The reality is that when you read horoscopes and then actually believe what your stars foretell, then you start attracting such events through the power of your thoughts. Here is an experiment you can try. Read what is written for all the 12 sun signs. Choose that sun sign which you like the most, i.e. which is the most positive for that day. Believe it will happen. And you will see that it actually happens. Thus you will realize that sun signs and horoscopes are nothing but a game of positive and negative thoughts.

12 THE WORRY LIBERATION MANTRA

The problem that is not grave enough to slay me can only strengthen me

The world is divided into two

Everything is created dually. Everything comes in pairs. Problems do occur in life. But they come with a lesson. If you do not learn the lesson that the problem brings along with itself, then the problem will repeat. Understand this rule of life through the following examples:

1. Along with examinations comes the fear of performance. Even if you somehow tackle the examination, but if you have not learnt to tackle your fear, then the fear lingers on. Next time, it comes back with greater intensity. Have you learnt to tackle your examinations and your fears?

2. When someone insults you, along with the insult, your ego is hurt. Even if you manage to make the person who insulted you to respect you, but do not learn to manage your ego, then your ego problem continues. Next time, your ego is hurt even more. Have you learned to manage both your insults and your ego?

3. Along with free time, comes boredom. Even if you manage to master your free time by doing something, but if you have not learnt to master your boredom, then you become a slave to boredom always. Next time, you are bored even more. Have you learnt to master both your free time and your boredom?

4. Whenever a problem occurs, stress (tension) follows. Even if you do solve the problem, but if you have not learnt to dissolve your stress, then you continue to be stressed. Even without problems, you will lead a stressful life. Have you learnt to both solve your problems and dissolve your stress?

Every problem is an examination

Take every problem that life throws at you as if it were an examination. The only question in the examination is, "In whatever you have learnt so far, are you progressing?" Once you ask this question, then problems do not appear as problems. That is why the worry liberation mantra reads as follows:

> **"THE PROBLEM THAT IS NOT**
> **GRAVE ENOUGH TO SLAY ME**
> **CAN ONLY STRENGTHEN ME."**

Thus if a problem does not kill you, it only makes you grow and learn more. Whenever a problem occurs, if you remember and repeat this mantra, you will find a great change in your attitude of looking at the problem. You will not be irritated by it and will actually start learning the lesson that the problem has brought along with itself.

Everyone says that you should learn from problems. But no one tells you how. When problems occur, they appear so big, that you forget to learn. The importance of the worry liberation mantra is that it automatically makes you learn from the problem once you repeat it. Whenever a problem occurs, all you need to do is to ask yourself, "Will this problem kill me?" If the answer is no, then it can only make you stronger. The moment you answer this question and know the mantra, you will start learning in order to grow stronger.

Application of the mantra

When your boss leaves you a message to see him urgently in his cabin, ask yourself, "Is this a problem grave enough to kill me?" If the answer is no, you will see that instead of worrying, you will go boldly into his cabin and face whatever situation has arisen.

When guests drop in unexpectedly and you are totally unprepared, ask yourself, "Is this a problem grave enough to kill me?" If the answer is no, then instead of becoming anxious, you will spontaneously manage the situation and learn from it and in the bargain have a great time with your guests too.

When you are stuck in a traffic jam and need to reach someplace urgently, ask yourself, "Is this a problem grave enough to kill me?" If the answer is no, then instead of getting tensed, you will find that you will learn to manage your stress in such situations.

Sometimes you may be running short of money. Sometimes you may be sick. Sometimes you may get into a fight. Whatever be the situation, however small it may be, by constant application of the mantra, you will find yourself growing stronger. Soon, you will be able to face any type of situation. Instead of wasting time worrying, you will spend the same time in learning and growing.

Every problem brings a gift

Gold has to undergo extreme heating in order to turn into pure gold. A diamond needs to be hammered, chiseled and polished before it becomes a diamond of value. Only by facing your fears can you become courageous. If you do not learn the lesson of facing your fears, the incidents that trigger fear will be repeated in your life until you learn the lesson. Every problem brings the gift of a lesson along with it and if you do not unpack the gift and learn the lesson, the problem will present itself again and again. If this is clear to you, then you will actually welcome problems rather than resisting current problems or worrying about future problems.

Repeat the mantra, learn the lesson, unpack the gifts and say hello to a beautiful life.

Increase your knowledge

The more you increase your awareness about life, the more you increase your level of consciousness, and the more you increase your knowledge, you will find worry automatically becomes meaningless for you. In the previous chapter, you saw that by increasing your knowledge about the meaning of problems, they do not seem as problems any longer. But that is only knowing a part of the whole. Increase your knowledge about the principles of life, about the ways of the cosmos, about the laws of nature. The more you become spiritually knowledgeable about how everything is being operated, worry automatically ceases.

Become more aware about God and His creation:

Has God intended trouble for man? Why are things the way they are? How everything has been created in abundance? Why are some poor and some rich inspite of everything being unlimited?

Become more aware about happiness and unhappiness:

Why is it that we feel more unhappy than actual unhappiness? Why is that we feel less happy than actual happiness?

Become more aware about false beliefs and notions :

What are beliefs? What are my beliefs? Do I believe I am the body? Who am I? Why am I here?

13. The Easiest Way to Be Rid of Worry
Know your instinctive mind

The mind can be divided into the intuitive mind and the judgmental mind. Also called the instinctive mind and the contrast mind respectively. When you are working and there are no thoughts interrupting your work, then you are working with the instinctive mind. Suddenly the contrast mind (the mind that contrasts constantly between good and bad) arises and comments on how great the work is going on. You become conscious immediately and work suffers. When you are working with your instinctive mind, you do not even notice how much time has passed. You have become one with your work. Scientists call it 'being in the zone' or 'being in the flow'. The contrast mind makes the impersonal instinctive work as personal work and corrupts the flow and gets you out of the zone.

Worrry is a product of the contrast mind (judgmental mind). When you are with the instinctive mind, you are in the present, in the moment. The moment you bring in your past or the future, then you are operating from the realm of the contrast mind. The whole secret is to be with the instinctive mind as much as you can so that you are always in the zone. To do that you need to understand on what premises do both these minds work. Following are the premises (foundations) from which the instinctive mind (IM) and the contrast mind (CM) operate:

IM : Work is impersonal. I have become one with my work.

CM : It is my work. It is very personal.

IM : I am neither interested in success nor in failure. Work is more important.

CM : I have to succeed. Success is good. I shouldn't fail. Failure is bad.

IM : I can only be in the zone. I cannot and need not experience spiritual truth or any feeling of enlightenment.

CM : I need to see it to believe it. I have to experience it and only then will I be convinced about the Truth.

IM : When you work, do the best you can.

CM : What if my work turns out to be bad? What If I fail?

IM : I will naturally avoid the mistakes that I have previously committed.

CM : Why do I commit such stupid mistakes?

IM : I need not see God or the Truth. I need not imagine how He looks, how It feels.

CM : How will God look like? How will It be like? Can I take it?

IM : Being in the present is happiness.

CM : What happiness have I attained in the past? What happiness will I attain in the future? Will I be happy at all?

IM : Whenever there is no work, there is no need to think.

CM : Nothing can happen without thinking. What will happen to all the work I have done so far? What work should I take up so that I can keep myself occupied?

IM : At one time, there is only one thing to do. Thus I am never burdened.

CM : There is so much to do. I have to complete so many unfinished things now. The entire burden is on me.

IM : Everything is happening spontaneously and automatically.

CM : I have to do things. Things are not happening properly. There is so much to do. I am great that I do all these things. I am stupid that I made some mistakes. Until I am sure of things, I won't even begin.

IM : Life is bliss, a dance, a demonstration.

CM : Life is happiness only after all my problems have been solved.

IM : All are one.

CM : I am separate from others.

IM : There is enough. Everything is abundant – love, money, happiness.

CM : Everything is scarce. There are lesser resources and more people.

So learn more about your contrast mind and instinctive mind. Learn to operate from your instinctive mind by being in the zone.

Work when you worry

When you are in danger, the body produces chemicals that fill the body with immense strength. When you see a lion in the forest ready to pounce on you, you run for your life. You are amazed as to how you could run so fast. The answer is simple – your body's flight mechanism produced chemicals and enzymes that gave it this ability. Your body is programmed to do that.

The problem is that your body does not understand the difference between reality and imagination. Thus, even if you are mentally worrying that a lion will pounce on you, the same chemicals are released. Thus, whenever you worry, you are creating mental images of danger. Your body reacts as programmed. It releases the chemicals required to spring the body into action. But you are sitting in your couch and making mental images. You do not actually run, as you would have if there was a lion preying on you. So the chemicals remain unused in the body. These chemicals then turn into toxins. These toxins then cause diseases. Thus, be it worry or fear, you are creating toxins in the body and growing more sick.

So the best thing to do whenever you worry is to get your body into action. Do some physical work whenever you worry or fear. Clean your house. Paint a picture. Exercise. Drink lots of water. The moment you do physical work, the chemicals released get used up. They do not convert into toxins. Doing physical work when you worry or fear is the most scientific advice one can ever give you.

The Final Way to be Rid of Worry
Increase your worries

You will learn a very unique way to vanquish worry in this chapter. This chapter will ask you to worry about the world. You might wonder how this will cure you of worrying. Let us explore how this is possible.

The Greatest Way to be Liberated from Worry

The greatest way to be liberated from worry is by increasing your worries. Increase your worries to such an extent that you now worry about the whole world. In the face of the worries of the whole world, your personal worries will seem miniscule. While bothering about all humanity and its problems, you will cease to worry about your small problems. Start creating miracles in other peoples' lives and your life will be full of miracles. In doing good for others lies your good. On doing good for others, the law of creation starts manifesting in your life.

The Law of Creation

The world is divided into two kinds of people. There are those who are the masters of life. And then there are others whom life is a master of. The first kind are those who are successful, who create and shape the events in their lives. The second kind are those who are unsuccessful and whose destinies are shaped by others. Ask yourself where do you fit in? Or do you belong to the third category. These are those who are indifferent. They are not complete failures, but neither are they totally successful. They are not extremely unhappy, but something or the other troubles them. They are constantly worried over something. You decide which category you belong to. Once you understand the power of the Law of Creation, you can't help being in the first category.

The law of creation is as old as humanity itself. The law of creation has been operating tirelessly from time immemorial. The law is constantly creating something, whether man understands it or not. The law operates on every facet of life. Once you understand the law, you can control it. Otherwise it is controlling you. There are three steps to master this law.

First Step : Understand the Law

The law simply states that every thought turns into reality. The moment you let powerful universal thoughts through your mind, the law starts working for you. All that has been divinely created starts to overflow in your life – love, riches, right goals, knowledge, wisdom. Through this law man can find happiness and thereby he starts sharing his happiness with others. He wants to help people. Only one who is content can help others. He starts worrying about the world and his minor worries vanish.

The moment you hear that all you need is to pass positive thoughts through your mind and you will start attracting those things as per the law of creation, you begin to doubt it. You think it can't be that easy. That is why you need to work on understanding this law. The best part of this law is that it works whether you believe it or not. Hence there is no harm in experimenting.

The law operates because the mind is interconnected to the river of consciousness. Your thoughts keep pouring into this river. Whatever you think, the river turns it into reality. The power of the river is unlimited. All that is needed is for your thoughts to be continuous. The law works because you are complete and perfect and are connected to Consciousness (God). You do not have all the results you seek in your life because you do not continuously think on those lines. Whatever you think and believe, you will create and act accordingly.

Second Step : Happy Thoughts

Having understood the law, you need to maintain a stream of happy thoughts. Repeat happy thoughts whenever you can. Repeat the thought: "God obeys man only when man obeys God. Man needs God for his energy and God needs man for his expression."

Whenever you are sick, instead of thinking negatively, repeat to yourself, "I am sick today because my thoughts are disconnected from the thoughts of the divine. Otherwise I am very healthy. Henceforth, I will let only divine thoughts pass through my body and mind."

Third Step : Surrendering

In the third step, surrender all your thoughts and aspirations to the law of creation — "The divine thinks rightly through me. These thoughts will manifest as per the law." Thus you can get on with your day to day work and leave the rest to the law. Whenever you doubt the law, remind yourself, "I am happy because everything is in the hands of the divine. I am convinced and content that the divine will take care of it."

Further you can even declare: "I am releasing my thoughts into the universe. The universe does not have problems (state your problem). I am no longer affected by this problem. I salute to the universal power which now guides me in every way. I surrender completely to its force."

The three steps mentioned above are proven. The more you elevate yourself through this, the more you start to worry about the world. This is the greatest way to be rid of worry.

You consider only your near and dear ones to be your family. Understand that the whole world is your family. Whatever you do to help the world will benefit you and give you immense happiness. To make yourself happy, elevate yourself through this law and make others happy.

How can you benefit from the three steps of Understanding, Happy Thoughts and Surrendering ?

The three steps mentioned in the above chapter are not just for curing worry. It is the same for all the miseries of life. The steps are the same for attaining the Final Truth too. Read the appendix pages at the end of the book which tell you about Tej Gyan Foundation, about Tejguru Sirshree Tejparkhiji and how Tej Gyan Foundation can through these three steps in the Maha Aasmani Retreat help you in your spiritual growth.

Self Liberation
Book Three : Anger

1 WHAT IS ANGER
Understanding anger and the defilements of the mind

Let us understand first what is the mind before we understand what is anger.

Definition of the mind

There are five main defilements or corruptions of the mind – lust, anger, greed, attachment and ego. The existence of mind is due to these defilements. Or it can also be said that because these defilements exist, the mind exists. Some also believe that because there is mind, that is why these five defilements exist.

Mind is unstable, always restless, and forever keeps on changing. If it is filled with jealousy in the morning, then it is filled with anger in the afternoon, with greed in the evening and confusion in the night. It is changing every moment. Sometimes it is sad and sometimes happy. Sometimes it is miserable, sometimes joyful. One moment it is filled with faith, the other with distress and doubts. Just now it was filled with reverence, now it is full of dishonesty. It was displaying compassion some time back, now it is filled with anger. Once it was ready to die for somebody, now it wants to kill that same person. This mind keeps on changing every moment. Therefore it just cannot be trusted. And we have become one with this ever-changing mind. We have become identified with this mind. This unstable mind is what we respect and trust.

Actually mind is an illusion. We will have to understand this mind. How was the mind created? Illusion means that which does not exist, but feels like it does. Mind does not exist, yet it feels like it 'is'. If you put a stick in water, it appears to be crooked or bent, but it is not crooked. It is like a rope that appears to be a snake in the dark. It is just because of darkness that the rope appears to be a snake, it is actually not a snake. Similarly because of ignorance, it appears that mind exists, but actually it does not. To understand this, we will have to see the mind in the light of knowledge.

The creation of the mind

The mind gets created because of our identification with it. As soon as we say that I am the body, I am the mind, the mind gets created. The moment we associate with the mind, it feels like 'I am the mind.' When we associate ourself with wealth, we feel 'I am wealthy'. When we associate ourself with a position, we feel, 'I am the Prime Minister.' When we associate ourself with religion, it becomes, 'I am a Hindu', 'I am a Muslim', etc. To whatever you add 'I', you become that. In a wedding, the moment you put the wedding ring on the bride, a whole set of relatives are suddenly born. You had no in-laws a few moments ago. The moment you put the ring, a long line of relations are born. Similarly, as soon as you said, 'I am the mind' – you have put a wedding ring around the mind. You have garlanded the mind. Now the relatives of the mind also become yours. There also it's a long line... lust, anger, malice, envy, rivalry, jealousy, confusion, sadness, joy, sorrow, friendship, enmity, anxiety, restlessness, success-failure... You get related to so many relatives.

The five defilements of the mind

Among these various vices, the five main defilements are – longing, anger, greed, attachment and ego. Longing or desire has been regarded as the most powerful weapon of mind. Mind derives its life from it. Continuously, the mind is giving rise to desires, and continuously desires are arising. And when desires are not fulfilled, it leads to anger. When a desire gets fulfilled, it leads to greed. Due to greed, when we start accumulating possessions, then arises the attachment for those things. And after acquiring possessions, arises ego. Thus this vicious cycle goes on.

What is anger?

Generally, it has been seen that when people get angry, they use bad language, they insult others, shout, scream or even get down to hitting. And if they are not able to do that, then they start throwing and breaking things. Their only intention is that by using any method, others should agree with them. If not, at least their displeasure should be expressed.

Anger means punishing ourself for others' mistakes. Whenever one sees another's mistakes, he gets angry. But at that time, he forgets that by getting angry he is punishing himself, torturing himself. Let us understand this through an example.

When we put a sugarcane into a sugarcane machine, the machine gets it sweetness first and later others get the benefit of the sweet juice. But if we put stones in that machine, then it will be the machine first that will get damaged. From this example if we consider our body to be that machine, then stones are the thoughts of anger, which will harm us first. If a person curses somebody, then it may or may not have a negative effect on the other. But certainly it will affect the person who is cursing.

Anger - a habit

Anger is a habit. In childhood there are no habits. Then one or two behaviours are repeated. As they are repeated, gradually they become a habit. When this habit is entrenched deeper, then it becomes a tendency. Tendencies are even deeper than habits. Due to a habit, a person may get angry even without any cause. Then due to the development of a tendency, he feels strange if he does not feel anger. It is very much possible to get liberation from the habit of anger. Initially, it might seem a little difficult, but even deep rooted tendencies can be uprooted. Every habit can be broken. Some habits may take a short time to break, some may take a longer time, but they can all be broken. The moment you understand that anger causes harm to the one who is getting angry, then it is easier to break this habit or tendency.

The relation between attachment and anger

Very often people consider anger as bad and attachment as good. But there is a deep relation between attachment and anger. Anger and attachment seem to be different, but actually are the two sides of the same coin. People desire freedom from anger but are not ready to relinquish attachment. People want to be rid of anger because anger comes cloaked in the blanket of hatred. However, they don't want to relinquish attachment since attachment comes cloaked in the blanket of love. Anger is offending, even disgusting and troublesome. But we have to get rid of both since both have the same age; one lasts as long as the other. Yet, attachment is acceptable to man. Actually attachment can be as bad since it leads to obsession. A mother is attached to her child. She thinks attachment is but natural. But then this attachment can turn into obsession. When her child falls sick, she starts crying. If her child doesn't eat, even she doesn't eat. This is obsession. Now she has begun to harm herself and thus compromise her ability to take care of the child. Only if she is healthy can she take proper care. But due to attachment, she feels that if my child has not eaten then I shouldn't eat too. In this way love changes into attachment. The gist is that attachment means clinging. Just like it is essential to get rid of anger, it is essential to be free from attachment too. Lesser the attachment and identification, lesser is the possibility of anger.

The relation between ego and anger

Ego and anger are two animals, one white and the other black. White does not feel as bad as the black one because white is subtle but black is prominent or obvious. In the same way, anger is obvious while ego is imperceptible. When somebody is angry, it can be clearly seen but an egoistic person's ego remains hidden. Here we have to understand that the cause and effect both lie within us. Ego is the cause and anger is the effect. Ego is subtle and so it cannot be seen. But anger is gross, so it can be seen. If somebody's ego is hurt, he gets angry. Anger is the symptom and ego is the disease.

The relation between compassion, love and anger

Anger and compassion are two polarities. Compassion is the opposite of anger. If we use the word 'love' instead of compassion, it reflects attachment to some extent. That is why compassion has been regarded as the opposite of anger. Compassion contains no attachment. Generally love and attachment are considered as being synonymous. Actually, there is no attachment in love, but there is attachment in obsession. Today, the definition of love is considered as attachment coupled with excitement. What I love, that should be mine. A personal attachment develops for it. If you see a bird flying in the sky, you feel love for it and you want to put it in a cage. Putting it in a cage is not love, it is attachment because love will want to set it free and not bind it. Seeing it flying free, love had arisen in your mind because love will be happy only to see it free. Attachment wants to take away its freedom. And when you cannot cage it, you feel angry. Attachment is the link between desire and anger. Improve your spiritual understanding about 'attachment' and how life is impersonal and liberate yourself not only from anger, but all the other corruptions of the mind; all of them arising out of attachment and identification.

A TALE OF ANGER

There was a small village where some monks used to go on their rounds for alms. One monk used to go every day to a lady's house asking for alms, where each day he would get some bread. After some days, that lady started getting angry on this monk – "Every day he comes and stands at my doorstep for begging!"

One day in a fit of anger, she put some poison in the bread and gave it to the monk. He took it and went away. In the late afternoon when the lady was busy with her work, the monk returned. He was carrying a dead body on his shoulder. The lady was shocked to see the monk alive. When he came near, she saw the dead body – she was stunned – that dead body was of her son. Her cries turned into screams when the monk told her that he had died because of eating some poisonous bread. This monk used to go every day to the jungle and if he met any hungry person, he would give a part of the bread to that person. That day in the jungle, he met this lady's son who was very hungry and hence the monk had given him the entire bread.

The purpose behind telling this story is to point out what one could lose owing to anger. How a small spark of anger can turn your life into ashes. There is no need to get so angry with someone that you want to kill him. It could have happened that this lady could have just refused to give any alms to the monk, but she became angry enough to take his life and lost her own son in the bargain.

Remember when you are in **anger** you are just one letter short of **danger**.

2 Types of the Angry
Find your type

Every man gets angry some time or the other in his life. There are different kinds of anger and different types of the angry. A pattern of anger emerges, which can be divided into the following four types.

The first type

These are the ones who are angry from inside and angry from outside too. In this type of the angry, thoughts are churning inside and the flames of anger are leaping outside. They are seething from within and exploding outside. They pass on their anger to others. They blame others. They are irritated at every small thing. Their mantra in life is that I am right and you are wrong. Unfortunately, they also think that this is the right way to live.

The second type

These are those who are angry from within, but calm externally. Understand this type through an anecdote.

A father was home babysitting his child. After some time, the child started wailing. The father began saying, "Cool down Robin. Don't get so angry

Robin. Anger is bad for your health Robin." He kept on saying all such things. When his wife returned, her neighbours reported to her, "Your husband was taking good care of your son Robin." The wife explained that Robin was not her son's name. It was her husband's name. That means he was pacifying himself! Taking his own name, he was trying to calm himself down since the child was wailing. This is the second type of the angry.

The third type

These type of people are calm from inside and angry from outside.

There was a snake that lived in a hole near a village. It used to trouble the people living in the village. Everyone was greatly distressed by this snake. The story goes that one day a hermit met the snake and advised it against biting and troubling others. The snake was transformed and stopped being angry and biting. When the children in that village came to know that the snake has now become harmless, they started hitting it with stones. The snake used to receive one beating or the other daily. It was almost on the verge of death. Then one day the hermit returned and was alarmed at the snake's condition. The snake complained that all this had happened because of his advice. The hermit then explained, "If you can't bite, you can at least hiss. Don't stop hissing."

The third type knows to hiss. Angry externally, but calm internally. They pretend to be angry when necessary.

The fourth type

These are those who are calm from inside as well as from outside. They don't even pretend to be angry.

Ask yourself, what type am I. These are progressive levels. Find out which level you are at and what is the recurring pattern of your anger. Contemplate on your type. Try to progress to at least the third or the fourth type.

Childhood and the Beginnings of Anger
The responsible way to rid your child of anger

There is no particular location of the origin of anger. We cannot locate that anger is arising from a specific place within the body. But one can say that man lives mostly in his head. His beliefs and notions arise from the head and govern his life. And it is these wrong beliefs and notions that give rise to anger. Hence we can safely assume that anger arises in the head. But the question is when did these notions and beliefs form? In childhood. So the origin of anger is in the head and the source is in childhood. The origin is in the head and the remedy is in the heart. The beginning is in childhood and the cure is in understanding your childhood.

Beginning of anger in children

When a child is small, he needs attention and protection. He gets that attention from his parents. In childhood, everybody looks after him and takes care of him. Whatever he wants, he gets. So unknowingly, he starts feeling that "I am the most important person in the world." However, he doesn't know that he is the weakest. That is why he is being given the maximum attention. In this way, the child mistakes his weakness to be his greatness. Under this wrong impression, he persuades others to fulfill his wishes, which later turns into obstinacy. Then if a desire of his is not fulfilled, he starts getting angry. "All my wishes are fulfilled, then why not this one?" This is how he misunderstands his weakness as his special quality.

The human child needs the most attention. If he is not given adequate attention, his survival is not possible. The young ones of animals don't need that much of attention; they grow on their own. That is why the feelings of anger, hatred, malice don't develop in them.

Gradually, the child learns how to use anger to get his necessities. But before learning anger, he learns to cry, he learns to speak, and then he sees how others use anger to get what they want. He listens to the language being used by his siblings and neighbours and he feels that this is the only way to get what he wants.

Look at your childhood now. Recollect the first incident when you threw a tantrum or cried. Can you recall an incident before that where you used your wails and anger? Can you recollect an incident before that? Can you see a pattern? Examine your relationship with your mother and father, or a significant influence in your childhood. Were they the ones who were using anger to get what they want? What did you pick from them? What did you learn from your parents when they were fighting or were angry? Just being aware of some of your habit patterns and the source of them in your childhood can easily set you free. You begin to realize that your predominant way of sucking energy from others is a decision taken in childhood. Your thinking that if I don't get angry, things don't get done, goes back to your childhood where you used to think that if I won't cry, things won't get done.

Good communication with children is the remedy

Now as parents, let us see what can we do to help our children to be free from anger. Parents are just as responsible for the child's anger as the child himself. When the child gets angry, the parents tell him, "You are so hot tempered. This is wrong." This induces a feeling of inferiority in them. They don't try to understand why the child is behaving in this manner. They never have any communication with the children. Very often, it happens that there is either no communication between parents and children, very less communication or very rare communication. In these circumstances, the children who are not able to communicate their feelings, express them through anger.

The most important thing a parent has to understand is that as their child is growing, their behaviour with them should change accordingly. When the child is small, their behaviour with him should be different. When the child has grown up, they should communicate with him in a different manner. As the children go on growing, their needs will go on growing. Learning will grow and many questions will arise in their minds. At times they won't get answers to some of their questions. Some of their desires may get fulfilled, some may not. Anger will increase due to unfulfilled desires. That is when parents need to communicate and explain about life. It can be stated that anger is lack of communication. Therefore it is essential that parents should learn the art of right communication with their children. This is critical for the growth of the child.

Alertness of Parents

When children get angry, parents can give them an understanding that, "You don't need to get angry. You can get what you want even without getting angry." Create an atmosphere in your home in which children have complete freedom of expression and where they can freely express their needs. This atmosphere will be conducive for forming a relation of friendship with children. It is essential that in every home there should be conversation and communication between parents and children every day. It should be made a part of routine daily activities, which will prove beneficial for the entire family. Misunderstandings will reduce, relationships will grow stronger, and there will be friendly behaviour with each other.

You can communicate only when you are alert. Parents have to be alert about what they tell their children when they get angry. Actually even anger is a method of communication. A person is expressing his displeasure through anger because he doesn't know any other method. If he learns the art of expressing himself through a different method, then he will feel that now he does not need anger. Hence parents have to be alert about the anger of their children, about the true feelings that are getting expressed in the form of anger. Then they should question the child about the true cause of anger. Explain to children that if you can develop the art of explaining your point clearly, then anger will be abolished. Anger is a feeling, a method to express the desires hidden inside us.

Anger with Awareness

Children learn anger primarily from their parents. If children see parents losing their self-control, they begin to think it is normal. Children are very perceptive. A child can perceive who loves him and who does not. A baby starts to cry if the person holding it is uncomfortable. Why, even dogs bark at those who are afraid of them! The human mind is powerful enough to perceive the intention of the other. If parents hit the child in rage, then children perceive that it is unnatural and incorrect. Therefore every parent should remember a simple rule. If you want to hit or scold your child, then do so with awareness. While you are angering over your child, tell yourself, "Now I am going to scold or hit him." This is anger with awareness. Children will perceive it as strictness and not the folly of the parent. If anger is involuntary, then children perceive that too. If you hit out in rage without any awareness and later try all the explanations in the world, it doesn't work. If, after hitting the child in a fit of fury, the mother tries to give explanations such as, "I hit him for his own good", then the child sees through the charade.

Parents can use anger with awareness. But, it should be used only when it is necessary. Anger is not always a disease. Sometimes, it is a necessity, a need of the hour. For example, if a child puts his hands on the stove, then there it is necessary to get angry. If you hit a child with awareness at that time, it will serve as a reminder and the child will not register it as your anger. Instead he will see it as his mistake. Some parents and teachers don't realize this. There have been cases where parents have hit their children with knives, have burnt their hands and so forth. Remember that awareness during anger is the best remedy for anger.

" In a survey, it was found that more than 80% of prisoners are repenting on their crimes. They said that a moment of anger had destroyed their lives. Anger is momentary madness.

4. The Aware Way to Be Rid of Anger
Understand the effects of anger

Anger is the lock

If man so desires, he can sow the flowers of joy or grow the thorns of anger. If he wants he can journey through hell or enjoy the pleasures of heaven. Heaven and hell are what you experience in life itself. When you get angry, you experience hell that very moment. The body can be a door to heaven. It can also be a door to hell. There are very few who know the art of how to make the body the door to heaven, the door to God.

If you think that only after you go to a pilgrimage you will get happiness and peace, then you are mistaken. Because the door to God or Heaven is not outside, but is within us. It is not at a future kingdom come date. It is here and now. An important pilgrimage site in India is Haridwar. Hari means God and Dwar means door. The whole point is that your body can become a Haridwar (a door to God). Anger is the lock on this door.

Understand that you don't get what you desire, but what you sow. You desire ambrosia, but you sow poison. When the fruits appear, they are of poison, of misery and suffering. It is amazing that man sows the seeds of anger and wants to have peace; sows the seeds of hatred and expects to reap love. He curses others, but hopes that everyone will bless him. This is impossible. Understand and get the knowledge of these simple laws of life. To every action, there is a reaction. This is the law of life. Every action will bring a reaction. If you curse somebody, then you throw a stone in the lake of consciousness. The ripples created due to the stone will go on spreading far and wide in the lake. At last they shall return to you. Be aware of the ripples you are causing.

Acceptance is the key

Along with awareness, a feeling of acceptance of others is critical. Acceptance is the key. Non-acceptance creates hell. Acceptance creates heaven. Even if somebody insults you, accept it. Somebody curses you, accept that too. And as a feeling of acceptance develops, then malice won't arise inside you, anger won't arise. Love will arise, compassion will arise. In this way, gradually, your body will start becoming the 'door to heaven'.

Awareness of destructive anger gets rid of anger

There are two types of anger. One is 'destructive' anger and the other is 'constructive' anger. Destructive anger can also be called as obstructive anger since it hampers the growth of a person due to which he goes in a negative direction. Its opposite is constructive anger due to which a person moves in a positive direction. 'Constructive anger' can be used for creative and formative purposes. Constructive anger is where there is exploration and new creation due to anger. Before understanding constructive anger, it is important to know destructive anger.

Destructive anger creates a vicious cycle. Let us understand this with the help of an example.

A company owner is on his way to the office. A dog bites him. He grudgingly goes to a doctor and therefore gets delayed for office. His work gets delayed. As a result, he gets angry. He lashes out at his manager. The manager cannot reply back to his boss. So the manager vents his anger on his secretary. The secretary in turn lets out her anger on the clerk. The clerk gets angry on the peon. The peon goes home and fights with his wife. The wife scolds her son. The son goes out and expresses his anger by hitting a stone at the same dog that had bit the company owner. Then the dog runs off to bite somebody else.

In this way, the vicious cycle goes on. This has a destructive effect on the family, the society and the nation. The environment in which our children are born and raised and the tendencies created thereof will definitely be imprinted in their minds. When that child grows up, he will lead a life made helpless by the habit of anger. In this way anger will have destructive effects not just on his body, but on his entire life.

Awareness of the negative effects

The aware way of being free from anger is to understand the negative effects of anger.

Physical effects

Medical research has proved that the cause of many illnesses is only anger and stress, particularly illnesses such as stomach ailments, sinus pain, headache, diabetes, high blood pressure, heart disease, insomnia, etc.

The causative factor for all these diseases is the stress on our nervous system, and this stress is created even more rapidly by anger. There is a gland in our brain called the pineal gland. Whenever we get angry, this pineal gland produces a particular type of chemical which is carried by blood circulation throughout the body, due to which this poison spreads in our entire body. This has adverse effects on every part of the body including the liver, the kidneys and the lungs. Even our heart gets affected by it.

Anger can create disease in that part or organ of the body which is weak or has less resistance. For instance, if somebody already has high blood pressure and he is getting angry, then there is a possibility of rupture of an artery in the brain which can also lead to paralysis.

Mental effects

Anger has drastic effects on the mind. An angry person usually suffers from mental diseases such as mental instability, depression, inferiority complex, insanity, etc. Doctors say that anger can even lead a person to the mental asylum because anger has a direct effect on the brain.

Social effects

Clashes in relations, break-ups in relations or fights with neighbors are often seen due to anger. In business also, most people don't like to deal with an angry person. Good workers also don't stay long with a boss who has an angry disposition.

The society which is infected by the disease of anger cannot progress. Such societies do not stay together during difficult times, do not help each other and even their financial growth is hampered. A person can even kill due to anger because there is a feeling of vengeance inside. In such a society, very often people kill each other in anger due to the flames of vengeance within. These societies are not even able to develop culturally. They are also not able to produce any outstanding literature because cultural development is a result of love, not of anger. Only a kind and loving society can create beautiful poetry and melodious music.

Spiritual effects

An angry person cannot walk the spiritual path. This is because an angry person will not be able to explore and investigate within himself. He will move away from himself due to anger. A multitude of problems will keep coming into his life. His life will be spent just in solving those problems. He will not have any time left for meditation, for spiritual discourses, or self- enquiry. As he solves problems angrily, he will create fresh anger and will become more and more entangled within it. Till the end of his life, this chain will continue and he will get more and more alienated from himself.

Destructive Anger in the world

The First World War, The Second World War, the Vietnam War, the Gulf War, the Taliban-Afghanistan War and many more conflicts. In just eight decades, more than eight major wars have been fought. The result – destruction, ruin, innocent people get killed, countless little kids become orphans, and many helpless women are widowed. Wars have given us nothing but destruction. In the Second World War, when the atom bomb was dropped on Hiroshima and Nagasaki, within a few minutes, millions were burnt to ashes.

If we take a look at history, we find that an exchange of a few words in anger have also led to wars. The mythological war of Mahabharata was a result of Draupadi's words, "Blind father, blind son." Words spoken with unawareness can result in massive destruction. There are various cases of friends fighting and nations warring because of anger or differences of opinion. Even today the fire of anger is blazing strong. That is why so many nuclear weapons are being invented; rockets, cannons and missiles are being produced. Scientists are saying that we have produced such an amount of nuclear weapons that can completely destroy 700 earths. We can kill each person 700 times. As if killing a person once is not enough!

This enormous increase in the number of killings is the result of anger.

> Attachment is the missing link.
> It is because
> you are attached to something
> that you crave for it.
> This leads to greed.
> If you get what you are greedy for,
> your ego increases.
> If you don't, it leads to anger.
> But it all started with attachment.
> Work on the missing link, the root cause,
> and anger will vanish permanently.

The Revolutionary Way to be Rid of Anger

Embrace, transform and use anger

Is there any use of anger at all?

Anger is not just destructive. Anger is nature's way of endowing us with energy. It depends on man as to how he uses this energy. Fire is energy. It can be used for cooking food and also for burning down homes. When homes burn, then we say fire is bad. Actually, it was the use of fire that was wrong and not the fire itself. In the same way, energy is neither good nor bad; it just depends on how we use it.

If energy gets directed towards love, then it is manifested as love. If it is directed towards anger, then it is manifested as anger.

The revlutionary way to be rid of anger

The revolutionary way to be rid of anger is simple – use your anger. Transform the destructive anger into constructive anger. If you learn to make constructive use of this energy, then you can be successful in getting constructive results even from anger. You will have to learn this art. Even in an extremely bad person, there are some good qualities. If you focus on those good qualities, then that person does not remain bad for us. Similarly, even with anger the doors of Truth can be opened.

If anger arises and sets us on the path of seeking the Truth or if anger arises and we start investigating, then this is investigative anger. A person is distressed by heat. He gets very angry and sets out to find such a thing which will end his distress. He then invents a fan. This is constructive use of anger. It is a misconception that anger is wrong. But the destructive use of anger is bad. Only destructive anger has negative outcome. History is proof that when there has been investigative anger, the outcomes have also been positive. Wherever the rulers of a nation or kingdom have exploited their subjects, those subjects have revolted in anger, creating a revolution. If there had been no anger in freedom fighters of colonized countries, perhaps their freedom would not have been possible. The anger aroused from patriotism was 'investigative anger' which some people expressed as violence, while some as non-violence. Violence and non-violence seem to be different but are the outcome of the same energy.

Science has done tremendous research in the field of energy and all the discoveries have been the result of investigative anger. Actually in order to understand investigative anger, we need an experimentative intellect and an open mind. We have been conditioned that anger has to be suppressed. Society has taught us to hold anger, suppress anger. But, understand that if you suppress anger within you, its results will be horrendous. Actually, people should be taught how to transform anger, how to create something from anger, how to benefit from investigative anger.

Due to anger, energy is produced in the body. The whole body vibrates with energy. That energy is not negative. Then as soon as the vibration created due to anger ceases, the person feels powerless. During the moment of anger, instead of acting against someone, engage yourself in some constructive work. Then you have learned to transmute and transcend anger.

How to transform destructive anger into constructive or investigative anger?

There is an instance in Saint Kabir's life where once he was appointed as a judge in a village. One day there was a theft in a wealthy person's house in that village. The thief was caught and brought before Kabir. When Kabir asked the thief why had he committed the theft, the thief answered that his mother was very sick and he did not have money for the medicine. He was helpless and that is why he had to steal. The thief was now supposed to be punished. But Kabir ordered punishment for three people. He ordered one day of imprisonment for the thief. Secondly, he ordered two days of imprisonment for the wealthy man since he had accumulated more wealth than required. Thirdly, Kabir punished himself with three days of imprisonment because in his village there was someone in such a pitiable condition and he did not even know it.

We have understood so far that anger is a manifestation of energy. When energy gets accumulated, then it needs a vent to come out. Whenever energy gets an opportunity, it takes a specific form and manifests itself. If water is poured into a glass, it takes the form of the glass. When poured in a pot, it takes the form of the pot. In the same way, energy is also manifesting itself in different forms – sometimes in the form of anger and sometimes in the form of love. So is anger a strength or a weakness? If we think beyond the polarities of good or bad, strength or weakness, a new understanding will dawn upon us. The understanding that anger is neither good nor bad. **'When you are using anger, it is strength and when anger is using you, it is weakness'**. This means that when anger is being used, as per the need of the situation with full awareness, then it is strength. But if you are getting angry just because the other person is also angry, then it is weakness. Reaction is weakness. Response is strength. When you are reacting to the situation without any awareness, it is a weakness, a folly. Responding with awareness as the situation demands is harnessing the strength of anger.

The most powerful form of revolutionary anger : Investigative Anger

A truth seeker's anger is the most powerful of all. It arises out of the question: "How much longer can I live in ignorance? Till when shall I burn in the fire of hatred and malice?" Because of these questions, his search begins. This is the use of investigative anger; even self- realization is possible. In the Buddha's life, the search for Truth had begun in this way.

When he saw an old person and a sick person, he asked his charioteer, "Am I going to be old too? Am I going to be sick too?" When he saw a funeral, he asked, "Am I going to die too? If I am going to die tomorrow, then today itself I have died." As a result, he left his home and family and set out in the search for Truth.

Anger of the Buddha

There is one more misconception in people's mind that a self-realized person does not get angry. Once it so happened that two of the Buddha's disciples were sitting and discussing about each other's begging bowls. They were discussing whose bowl was more beautiful. The Buddha heard their conversation and shouted at them, "You have come here after renouncing your home and family and everything else. But, even after coming here if you are doing the same thing that you used to, then what is the use of all this? Even today you are seeing beauty in external objects. If you want to find beauty, then search for it inside yourself."

The wise don't get angry. They create anger for the benefit of others. They create it with full awareness.

6. The Knowledgeable Way to Get Freedom from Anger

Know the cause, remove the effect

Anger is the outcome of man's internal weakness. There are seven causes of anger. Once you know the cause, the effects can be controlled and even eliminated.

The first cause : The habit of desire

Desire in itself is not the cause of anger. The habit of desire is the cause of anger. The tendency to create another desire the moment one desire is fulfilled is the root cause. Instead of sitting peacefully, as soon as man gets some free time, he thinks, "What do I get now?" This habit is the block in his spiritual progress.

A very rich man was showing off his property to his friends. He proudly displayed three swimming pools in his mansion. "The first pool always contains hot water, I bathe in this pool in the winters. The second pool always contains cold water, I bathe in this pool in the summers ", he proudly announced. The on-looker asked, "Why the third pool? It doesn't even have any water." The rich man replied, "On some days, when I don't feel like bathing, then I go and sit in this pool."

The mind has developed the habit of desires. Man begins with small things. He wants to become something. But even after becoming something, he wants many things. Now giving rise to desires has become a tendency with him. If somebody gets in the way of his desires, then he will get angry. Because of this habit, he will continue getting miserable and will continue getting angry.

The second cause : Hurdle in desires

Every man has some desires. Some desires are strong and some are subtle. Everybody can understand strong desires such as getting success, getting a job, passing an exam, and so on. But subtle desires can be understood only after something happens. If the power (electricity) goes off and you get angry, that means you had a subtle desire that there should be power. You get angry on the people working at the power station. You curse them. Thus even hurdles cause anger. But that too is nothing other than the tendency to desire. Things are going on fine, you don't think you are angry. When something is obstructed or goes wrong, then subtle desires manifest and cause anger.

The third cause : Attachment to senses

Because of attachment with senses, desires arise. Because of unfulfilled desires, anger arises. The desire to accumulate wealth also arises because of attachment to senses. Wealth can provide something for the senses. We can buy a TV with money and TV can show beautiful sights to our eyes. Money can buy a music system so that our ears can listen to music. Desire to collect wealth beyond our needs arises as a result of our attachment to senses. Every desire is connected to the senses.

Guru Nanak did not ever keep money with him. It was not because he had renounced money. The fact is that he did not have any desire or wish to satisfy his senses.

The point is not that one should not want money. The point is that everything you want is for the senses. Just become aware of this. You can desire for all the money you want as long as you do not forget the treasure within yourself. In spite of all the money in the world, can you lead a simple life? The more you get habituated to the comforts that amenities provide, the more will be the possibility for inconvenience if you don't get those amenities. And inconvenience becomes the cause of anger. When an object is taken away from us, we get angry. That is why very often wealthy people suffer from the disease of anger. They get angry at every little thing. Often they get angry on their servants. They get angry on their wife and children. Understand and know that objects can give convenience, not contentment. There is a difference between convenience and contentment. Know that there is no permanent happiness in satisfying the senses. This will be possible only when you realize and understand with experience that, "I am not the senses." Then attachment to senses can break.

The fourth cause : Anger fuels you

All the people in the world know that anger is bad. Everybody is distraught with the outcomes of anger. Nobody likes to get angry. Yet they get angry some time or the other in their lives. Everybody wants to get rid of anger, but are not able to relinquish it because they get something from it. A person feels alive with anger and gets freedom from boredom. Nobody wants to get bored; nobody wants to feel lifeless. But you get bored. So now you want some energy, some thrill, some excitement. Anger provides all of these. That is why you think it's a good bargain. Remember that, in fact, it's a very bad bargain. Anger gives only temporary excitement. But it will cause pain to other people as well as yourself. And by making a habit out of this, you will be troubled by it all your life.

A car is filled with fuel. It starts running. Similarly, when a person gets the petrol of anger, his body gets vibrations of excitement. He feels alive for some time. This is the reason that in spite of knowing that anger is bad, you don't relinquish it.

The fifth cause : Hurt ego

When the ego is hurt, anger arises instantly. When it seems that someone has insulted you or hasn't given you respect, you burst out into anger. Ego is the feeling of 'I' and 'Mine'. It's due to ego that a person feels that he is separate from others. Due to ego, he is never able to love anybody. He constantly fears that somebody may snatch 'mine' from me. That's why he doesn't allow anybody to come close to him. There are many who till the end of their lives believe that 'I am better than others. Others are inferior to me and I am entitled to be respected.' If he gets insulted, his ego is hurt and he gets angry.

Some people have a fragile ego due to which they get enraged very easily. Fragile ego means that ego which gets hurt with every little thing, every undesirable word and every wish that is not fulfilled. To protect his ego, he takes the help of anger. Instead of bending down to a fragile ego, break it completely. (You don't need any weapon to break your ego. Bright Understanding or Tejgyan can dissolve it completely).

In fact, ego is the root cause of anger. We feel hurt because of ego, which gives rise to malice. Malice gives rise to hatred. Hatred gives rise to anger. Anger leads to wrong deeds, and wrong deeds give rise to guilt.

The sixth cause : Guilt

Man is filled with guilt and because of guilt he hates himself and denies himself. A person filled with guilt will also hate others. The one who doesn't love himself cannot love others. Only a person filled with inferiority complex searches for 'status' (position, acquisitions, etc.) since he doesn't know the 'Ultimate Status'. If such a person achieves some status in life, he will only make others miserable. He will exploit people, harass people, trouble and torture people and will constantly keep getting angry.

The seventh cause : Formula made in ignorance

Children are weak in their childhood. As such, to get their own way, they develop a formula, which they feel is a success formula. To get something done from others, they will get agitated, stamp their feet, injure themselves or others and trouble themselves. They create a formula of being angry and getting things done. The child feels that everybody will get scared and fulfill my wish. The parents and other family members don't want to see their child in such a state. Therefore they agree with everything he wants. And this becomes a success formula for the child. Now the child has grown up. There is no need to use the formula. But in ignorance, the formula continues.

> The external world is an expression of God, it is not for troubling us. Similarly, anger is not for troubling us. Anger is also a different type of expression of life.

THE PREPARED WAY TO BE RID OF ANGER
Ten measures to get rid of anger before anger arises

People think about the remedy for anger after getting angry. Ideally it should be that before anger arises, the remedy for anger should be found. That is why in daily routine life, keep practicing tolerance and patience. With the development of tolerance, anger immediately reduces. This book is the cure for anger before anger arises. Reading it repeatedly, contemplating on it and following its instructions is the remedy. After getting sick, people often think about exercise. But, a wise man starts exercising before falling sick. The wise don't dig a well after feeling thirsty. Instead even before thirst arises, they make proper arrangements for water. Practice the following measures to get rid of anger even before anger arises.

1. Be receptive and attentive

Develop the habit of being in complete silence and peace every day for 15 minutes any time of the day. Keep the body steady. Fill your mind with happy thoughts and maintain slow rhythmic breathing.

Observing complete silence may not feel

comfortable or enjoyable. But these 15 minutes shall teach you a lot. For the first time, you will be able to know your mind and its games. And getting free from wrong beliefs and notions, you will receive the blessing of peace. You can also meditate.

2. Take deep breaths

Make it a habit that with every thought of anger, you shall take a deep breath. Whenever you get a negative thought, take a deep breath and release it slowly. This habit will be beneficial for diffusing your anger as well as it will be good for your health.

3. Take a balanced diet (Like food, like mind)

Your mind is what you eat. Your mind becomes just like the food you eat. If your body is filled with spicy or heavy and cold food, then accordingly the mind within the body will also become restless or lazy and indolent. If your body is filled with balanced and light food, then the mind within the body becomes active, sharp, focused and calm. There is a deep relationship between the body and the mind. Don't consider them as two separate entities. Consider it as one body-mind mechanism. Right from today, start analyzing the food being put in your body and make your mind strong and powerful. A balanced person eats such type of food that allows equal amount of blood flow from the heart to the stomach and from the heart to the brain. Always remain a little hungry. Don't completely stuff yourself. Take less and balanced diet. Balanced diet is helpful in keeping the mind stable. In a stable mind, the fire of anger does not arise.

4. Get freedom from anger by exercise and other physical activity

The more you are physically fit, the more will your anger be employed in increasing your strength and completing your work.

5. Keep faith in the principles of life

Every creature of this earth has been created to lead a healthy life and to make progress. Keep complete faith in this rule. Anger is a conspiracy against nature and the laws of nature.

Make this a principle in your life: "Below one roof, two people shall not get angry at the same time." This means that when your sister or brother, mother or father, wife or husband are expressing their anger, at that time, you don't have to get angry. By following this rule, you can prevent many problems at home which arise due to anger. When out of two people, one controls his anger, then the other cannot continue his anger for long. When you make one rule and follow it, you will know the power of making principles in life.

6. Read spiritual books

The words of Tejgyan (Bright Knowledge) are your true companion. Your anger-filled mind can be controlled through the spiritual resources of Tej Gyan Foundation. Read spiritual books. Read religious books regularly and with full faith.

7. Listen to the truth

Make it a habit to attend spiritual discourses. Attend Satsang (the company of Truth) at least once a week. The words of Truth will eliminate the darkness of fear, depression, anger, and will spread the light of peace in your life.

8. Don't use words that provoke anger

Don't tell someone that you are looking sick and tired. Or that you always make mistakes. Your words may become the cause of anger or the root of disease for that person and for yourself.

9. Express your mind's desire

Express freely and honestly what is in your mind and the reason for your anger to a well-wisher. This will help to cool down the flames of your anger. (Not being able to express your mind inflames anger).

10. Learn to forgive others

Learn to forgive others as well as yourself. If you forgive others, then are you not doing a favour on them. It's a favour by you on yourself. Do yourself a favour. Learn to forgive others.

> Anger leads to lack of awareness.
> Lack of awareness gives rise to wrong beliefs and notions,
> Wrong beliefs and notions make us
> forget our true nature.

8. THE COOLEST WAY OF CALMING ANGER
Prayer – The blessing of peace

If anger is burning coal, then prayer is cool water. The words of prayer cool down the burning of the whole body. On praying, a person's receptivity for peace increases. That means he allows peace to enter inside him. Peace fills his whole body, his whole life. It proves to be a blessing, a boon.

For calming the flames of anger, sing the prayer given below from within, with awareness and love.

I am peaceful in the presence of God (Silence).
I am experiencing complete peace.
I am created by God,
Therefore tranquility, peace, and happiness,
which is the nature of God
is spreading within my heart and mind.
God has created nothing to disrupt this peace.
Whatever may be the reason of my instability,
it is not in the list of the Almighty.
I am offering myself in his lap,
just like a tired child rests in the lap of his mother.

Waves of happiness are arising all around me and I am feeling a sense of stillness everywhere.
Peace…Peace…Peace…

The above is the shortest method to get freedom from anger. In this method, you just have to repeat this Truth, this prayer, again and again. The words of Truth can liberate you from anger easily.

> There is no need to live scowling with anger. It is necessary to let out the air. It is necessary to laugh and live.

9   Eight Quick Fire Measures to Calm the Fire of Anger

Temporary measures

The following are some temporary measures that will provide immediate relief when you feel angry:

1. Postpone

Almost everybody is an expert at postponing things to the next day. Instead of postponing your tasks, you can postpone your anger. If you need to be angry, tell yourself, "I will express my anger tomorrow." Decide to do so and abide by your decision. If anybody has sweared at you or insulted you, then you must postpone your reaction to it. Give a delayed response. This delay is an effective and sure remedy to pacify the flames of anger.

2. Think about the consequence

Everyone spends a lot of time thinking about their eating habits. But hardly anybody spends time thinking about their thinking habits. Everyone thinks about what they are feeding their body with. But nobody thinks about what they are feeding the mind with and what is the consequence of what they are harbouring in their mind.

At the onset of anger, if you just become aware of the possible consequences of you raising the roof, then anger can be controlled easily. Cultivate the habit that whenever you are angry, you will ask yourself the following question: "What are the negative consequences of my anger?" This will help you get rid of anger.

3. Speak softly

Research has proven that if one speaks loudly or shouts, then the propensity of anger increases. Conversely, if you speak softly, then anger reduces. Extending this, whenever a person is angry with you, then you must speak softly. This will help in controlling your anger as well as the other person's anger. It is difficult to do so, but not impossible. People have always encouraged anger. A is angry. He speaks to B in a loud voice. B retorts back loudly. A is angrier now, so is B. All that has to happen is the reverse. As B starts to speak softly, A's nerves too calm down.

4. Look into a mirror

Look into a mirror whenever you are angry. By looking at your facial expressions which is not your usual self, you will become immediately aware and not wish to be angry. You will not like your own face. You can also look at a mental mirror. Whenever you feel angry, ask yourself the question, "How am I looking at present?" You will become aware instantly.

5. Drink cool water

Drink cold water when you get angry. It has been observed that when one is angry, there is heat produced in the body. By drinking water, the body heat will be reduced and anger will be pacified.

6. Count some numbers

Count numbers from one to ten and again backwards from ten to one whenever you are angry. By counting numbers, specially backwards, the focus of the mind shifts from anger to something else. Hence this works as a temporary effective measure.

7. Utilize the power of words

When angry, you can repeat some affirmations or chant some 'mantra'. You need not say them out loudly, yet see to it that there is movement of the speech organs. This will enable you to get rid of anger very quickly. An affirmation that is suggested is: "I am cool, calm and composed."

8. Utter the name of God

The other thing you can do is to utter the name of God or your Guru when in anger or visualize Him in front of you. This should give rise to devotion and hence anger will vanish.

" There are some people who sometimes get angry and there are some people who only sometimes don't get angry. That means they are always angry. "

10 Seven Sure Ways to Get Rid of Anger

1. Relaxation

Stress is a gradual consequence of anger. If the mind is tensed, it will certainly lead to anger. Relaxation will relax your body as well as your mind; it is akin to meditation. This meditation could be done either by sitting or lying down. It is more easier to do it by lying down.

Either sit or lie down. Focus your attention on every part of your body from the toes to the forehead. Wherever there is stress in the body, give a mental instruction to that part to loosen up. Give an instruction that the body is getting relaxed and stress-free. The moment you give this mental command, that part of the body will get relaxed. Move to the next part. Your body and mind will get relaxed through this meditation and it is difficult to get angry in a relaxed state of mind. Where there is no stress, there cannot be anger.

2. Concentrate on the ten states of mind and the breath

An important solution has been provided in 'Yoga' which helps in controlling anger. What yogis noticed is that the rate of breathing increases when you are angry. Hence, according to Yoga, if you are successful in controlling your breath, then it will be difficult for you to continue to be angry. In order to control your breathing, take deep breaths. If you succeed in doing so, then you can control your anger.

To control anger, control your breath. What is even more beneficial is to just watch and be aware of the changes in your breath in all states of mind, not just anger alone. All that you have to do is to observe the state of your mind at any given moment. Given below are ten anchors. Against each of them, become aware of the changes in your breath. What happens to your breath with A? With B? and so forth.

- **A-** **Anger :** When angry, observe the rate of your breathing, whether it is slow or fast. Also observe how your breath has lost its rhythm.

- **B-** **Boredom :** Boredom is a great sickness these days. After the age of 3, even a child starts saying that he is bored! The whole idea of everything that happens in society is to escape boredom by engaging in one form of excitement or the other. When you are getting bored, instead of going out, all you have to do is to go within and observe what is happening to your breath.

- **C-** **Confusion :** When you are in trouble, you fail to understand what should be done and what not. Observe your breath at this stage and the mind settles down and everything becomes clear.

- **D-** **Depression :** Observe the changes in your breath when you are sad or worried.

- **E-** **Ego :** Your ego may get hurt due to some incidents. And then starts a series of conversations with self. Instead, just observe what happens to your breath.

F- **Fear** : Every person is afraid of something in his life. Fear, be it small or big, does affect the breathing. Continue to study your breath when you feel scared.

G- **Greed** : Note your breath when you develop a greed for something.

H- **Hatred** : Switch to the awareness of your breath the moment you harbour thoughts of hatred for someone.

I- **Illwill** : If you intend to harm anybody, switch your attention to your breath. This will prevent anger from arising.

J- **Jealousy** : With the advent of jealousy, your breathing loses its rhythm. Become alert towards this.

3. Increase your willpower

A person who does not have willpower will definitely lack in self-confidence. The one who has no self-confidence can never get rid of fear or anger. He will always remain scared and lead a life of fear. He will always harbour the fear of failure. He may get frustrated or disappointed with anything and everything. Due to this fear, he will get irritated and thus angry at every minor thing. Thus a vicious cycle begins. To come out of such a vicious cycle, one should improve his willpower.

Every person makes promises to himself and to others. He is unable to fulfill them. And willpower starts to diminish. Therefore, as the first step, do not make a promise that you cannot keep up. If you have made a resolution, you must fulfill it. Thus begin with small resolutions. E.g.: I shall keep my hand raised in the air continuously for 2 minutes. I will not bring it down before the end of 2 minutes. Or I will study for 2 hours. I will not move from here. I will not have my lunch today. Fasting is a very good experiment to increase your willpower.

As these smaller resolutions get fulfilled, you could take upon bigger ones and add to your self-confidence.

You could perform another experiment before you go to sleep. When you hit the sack, ask yourself, "Is there one more task that I can complete before I go to sleep?" Go ahead and complete it. Even if the task is trivial and not urgent, complete one such task every day. If you do so, you will find your willpower increasing tremendously.

Practice all the above and increase your willpower to ultimately get liberation from anger.

4.   Choose and get angry

Do not get angry always in the same manner. People get angry, scream and destroy things in the same manner as they have always been doing. This technique suggests you to get angry but with a difference and a novelty in it. Adopt a different manner of getting angry every time you feel anger. By expressing your anger creatively, you can influence people around you to a great extent. Think and write down some ways of getting angry and choose one of them when you get angry the next time. Man is choosing something or the other every moment of his life. Now, choose the manner in which you shall express your anger.

A teacher used to teach children that their clothes should be clean, shoes ought to be polished, and so on. But his students seldom practiced what he preached. One fine day, he expressed his anger, but uniquely. He himself got a brush and a shoe-polish and sat outside the classroom door and announced: "I am going to polish the shoes of the students whose shoes aren't clean." The students were shocked. Some started crying. They learnt their lesson and promised never to have unpolished shoes again.

It is not an easy task to express anger creatively. It needs courage. It needs you to choose. There are times when you do need to express your anger. But let it be your choice, not arising out of compulsion.

5. Stop getting angry on anger

Getting angry on anger is the real cause of misery. Man is suffering because of what is called as dual anger. Say you are upset about something. And then you are feeling upset over being upset. This is what is termed as dual anger. Another example could be when the body is in pain. When the body is in pain, the mind is upset over the pain and raises questions such as, "Why do I have pain?", "Why me?", "When will I be relieved of this pain?" and so on. Such pain over pain is multifold pain. The body was in pain. The body was being treated. The body is capable of handling and healing the pain. Nature has endowed the body with healing power. But the mind made this pain as "my" pain and aggravated the pain. First stop getting angry about anger to completely eradicate anger.

Let us understand this with another example. You felt angry. There is no problem with that. Look at a child in anger. It is angry one moment and the next moment it is playful. But when you are in anger, you tend to create 'anger' over anger — "Oh, why do I have so much anger!" "I shouldn't get so angry." "I am frustrated at my lack of self-control." Even after the bout of anger is over, you tend to dwell on it for hours together. This is precisely the problem. Thus it is anger over anger that upsets the mind. The more you understand this, the more easily you will be able to get rid of double anger.

Going forward, whenever you feel anger, remember these steps:

1. Accept your anger first. "Yes, I am feeling angry."

2. There is no need to be angrier about being angry. "Anger on anger" is the result of ignorance.

3. When there is no anger on anger, then it will be fairly simple to get rid of anger.

4. Repeat to yourself that now that this anger has arisen, there is something I need to act upon. This action ultimately leads to my growth.

5. Whenever there is anger, it would have left you with a lesson — a lesson of understanding. A lesson that would have taught you the art of being calm and peaceful even while in anger.

Not only can you use the five steps mentioned above for anger, but also for fear and worry.

6. Laughing

A laughing person will never be able to get angry. A sad and sick mind alone can produce anger. A laughing person does not take seriously any situation that can provoke anger. He finds every situation quite okay and takes every situation in his stride with ease. The habit of laughing makes one pure. It cleans away the dirt of the past and gives a new point of view. Laughing makes a person feel alive, energetic and creative. Medical science today claims that laughing prevents many diseases. During the course of a disease, if a person is able to laugh, then his recovery is faster. Anger itself is a disease and laughing can prove to be a sure medicine for its cure.

Even today therapists are treating so many mentally ill patients using laughter therapy. If you start the day with a laugh then you will feel so many tensions easing away. Laughter in the morning can save you from being grim throughout the day. It's a simple and beautiful start to the day. Just like we take three meals in a day, similarly if we are able to simply laugh without any cause, then the thrill of happiness will run through us the whole day and we will feel that anger is miles away from us. If we rise and laugh in the morning then we will feel like laughing throughout the day.

7.   Who is feeling the anger

One thinks a lot about the question, "What is the solution for anger?" Instead ask a new question, "Who is feeling the anger?" Then the truth shall arise. As soon as anger arises, we have to remember that whom are we getting angry at, who is the other person, and who is getting angry? This is the process of self-enquiry. Doing this honestly is the key.

In this method, you have to ask that who is feeling anger – the body, the mind or you? When you are standing on the shore, your reflection falls on the water. When the water starts moving, even your reflection begins to move. Seeing this, if someone tells you, "You are moving", then you will reply, "My reflection is moving, not me. Any movement of my reflection makes no difference to me. Whatever is happening, is happening with my reflection."

When you understand this truth, you find out that I am not feeling anger, it's my mind that is feeling the anger. If you are given an object to use, then you use that object. You don't become that object. If you are using a microphone, you don't become a microphone. If you are using a car, you don't become a car. In the same way, you are using your body-mind mechanism. You are not the body-mind. When you will find this truth, you will realize that whatever is happening is happening with this body-mind mechanism. Anger is a delusion. Whenever anger arises, see who is feeling anger. 'You are separate from anger'. When you will know this by experience, a great change will occur in your life. Then you will realize that there is no need to get angry. Now you are feeling so lively that you don't need any fuel from outside. Right now close your eyes and check your feeling; the good feeling you have within you. This is the feeling of life. It is your being. You have just forgotten to feel that. So somebody should remind you again that life is within you, which you are searching outside. If you realize this, then you will start getting happiness (fuel) from within yourself. Then you won't need to feel alive by fighting with others.

> In the court of Intellect, When Anger sits on the throne, then the minister of Discrimination (reasoning) runs away.

11 THE ULTIMATE WAY TO BE RID OF ANGER
The anger liberation mantra

This is the last remedy for anger. Until now we have increased our awareness and understood temporary and permanent preventative measures for anger. The most powerful of all methods is to use the anger liberation mantra. It is actually a question. The question is: "Exactly what's happening?" When you feel anger, what is exactly happening? When you start observing this, you will find that there is heat generated in your body due to anger. Your heartbeats are faster. Just acknowlege what is hapenning. When anger arises, there are some signals in the body such as:

1. Faster breath.
2. Redness of face.
3. Clenching of fists.
4. Redness of eyes.
5. Higher pitch of voice.
6. Trembling of body.
7. Stuttering of tongue.

Acknowledge all these and any other symptom on your body. As soon as you focus your attention on a part, the sympton or vibration present in that part disappears. This experiment will have two results. Firstly, anger will be transformed into awareness. Secondly, when you will search for anger within you, you will find that anger is simply not there. In this way you escaped the consequences of anger and anger was used creatively. In addition to that you also became aware. Now your understanding of anger has improved. Gradually you will develop this habit and then it will become very easy for you. Freedom from anger will not appear to be a big problem. Now you won't say, "I am feeling angry." Instead you will say, "My heart is beating faster or there is a vibration in these parts of my body or there is just some pressure sensation on this part."

Anger is a disease of the mind, and awareness is its remedy. If anger is seen with awareness, then anger disappears. There is no need to fight with anger; instead you need to understand it with awareness. This is a very simple but effective technique, you can achieve total liberation from anger with this technique.

With this experiment, you will have heightened level of awareness. After that, whenever you will feel anger, you will know it with awareness. Even before getting angry, you will know it. Before anger arises, as soon as the breathing becomes faster, you will become aware. It will be impossible to get angry with consciousness because anger is the result of ignorance. The right knowledge is a sure remedy for anger.

So, if you want your anger to disappear, ask yourself:

Exactly what's happening?...

www.ingramcontent.com/pod-product-compliance
Lightning Source LLC
Chambersburg PA
CBHW070910080526
44589CB00013B/1250